# Talk Russian

## Svetlana Furlong
and
## Georgina Martin

**Series editor**
**Alwena Lamping**

Published by BBC Active, an imprint of Educational Publishers LLP,
part of the Pearson Education Group
Edinburgh Gate, Harlow, Essex CM20 2JE, England.

First published 1998.
Revised 2005.
Tenth impression 2011.

ISBN: 978-0-563-52027-6

Project Manager: Alexis Chung
Project Editor: Tamsen Harward
Edited by Anne Gibbens
Design management by Book Creation Services
Design by Avril Broadley for BCS
Illustrations by Sylvie Rabbe and Beatriz Waller for BCS
Typeset by Gene Ferber for BCS
Cover design by Helen Williams and Matt Bookman
Cover photograph: Getty Images/Image Source
Audio producer: John Green, tefl tapes
Sound engineer: Tim Woolf
Presenters: Larissa Kouznetsora, Leonid Osokin, Irina Shumovitch,
Stanislav Suknenko
Studio: Robert Nichols Audio Productions
Music by: Peter Hutchings

Printed and bound in China (CTPSC/10)
The Publisher's policy is to use paper manufactured from
sustainable forests.

# Contents

# Introduction

Welcome to **Talk Russian**, BBC Active's Russian course for absolute beginners. Designed for adults learning alone or in a class, it provides the ideal introduction to Russian, covering the basic language needed in everyday situations on a visit to Russia (and indeed many Baltic states). It is suitable if you want to learn for work, for fun and to prepare for a first level qualification.

**Talk Russian** is an interactive course consisting of a book and two 60-minute CDs of recordings made by native Russian speakers. Although designed to be used with the CDs, the book could be used separately as the audio scripts are included in the reference section. Free tutors' support and activities are available online at www.bbcactivelanguages.com/talk.

**Talk Russian** encourages you to make genuine progress and promotes a real sense of achievement. The key to its effectiveness lies in its structure and its systematic approach. Key features include:

- simple step-by-step presentation of new language
- involvement and interaction at every stage of the learning process
- regular progress checks
- useful hints on study skills and language-learning strategies

## How to use Talk Russian

Each of the ten units is completed in ten easy-to-follow steps.

1   Read the first page of the unit to focus on what you are aiming to learn and to note any key vocabulary in the 'В России . . .' *(In Russia . . . )* section. This provides useful and relevant information on Russia and sets your learning in context.

2   Listen to the key phrases – don't be tempted to read them first. Then listen to them again, this time reading them in your book too. Finally, try reading them out loud before listening one more time. In the first four units new words and phrases have been transliterated (written in English letters).

3   Work your way through the activities which follow the key phrases. These highlight key language elements and are carefully designed to enable you to complete them without

needing to write any Russian. When you hear the activity number pause the CD and read the instructions before you listen. If you wish to write Russian, try to copy the handwritten alphabet given in the pronunciation guide. To check your answers, refer to the *Audio scripts and answers* starting on page 101.

4   Read the 'По-ру́сски . . .' (*In Russian . . .* ) explanations – they are placed just where you need that information.

5   When you have completed the activities, and before you try the *Put it all together* pages, close your book and listen to the Russian conversations straight through. The more times you listen, the more familiar the language will become. You might also like to read the dialogues at this stage.

6   Complete the consolidation activities on the *Put it all together* page and check your answers with the *Audio scripts and answers*. In the first four units these activities are specifically designed to help you to learn the alphabet. In Russia, printed styles can vary – you should be able to recognise most versions.

7   Use the language you've learnt – the presenters on the CDs will guide you through the *Now you're talking!* page as you practise speaking Russian.

8   Check your progress. First, test your knowledge with the quiz. Then check whether you can do everything on the checklist – if in doubt, go back and spend some more time on the relevant section. You'll have further opportunities to test your knowledge in each 'Контро́льная рабо́та' (*Checkpoint*) after units 4, 7 and 10.

9   Read the learning hint at the end of the unit for ideas and suggestions on how to use your study time effectively or how to extend your knowledge.

10   Finally, relax and listen to the whole unit, understanding what the people are saying in Russian and taking part in the conversations. This time you may not need the book.

**Жела́ем успе́ха!** Good luck!

# Pronunciation guide

Russian is heavily stressed and the pronunciation of a vowel may change depending on whether it is stressed or unstressed.

Notice the difference between the printed and handwritten versions of the alphabet.

| Printed | Handwritten | Pronunciation |
|---|---|---|
| Аа | *Аа* | a in **a**pple |
| Бб | *Бб* | b in **b**ox |
| Вв | *Вв* | v in **v**an |
| Гг | *Гг* | g in **g**et |
| Дд | *Дд* | d in **d**og |
| Ее | *Ее* | ye in **ye**t |
| Ёё | *Ёё* | yo in **yo**ur |
| Жж | *Жж* | s in plea**s**ure |
| Зз | *Зз* | z in **z**oo |
| Ии | *Ии* | ee in f**ee**t |
| Йй | *Йй* | y in bo**y** |
| Кк | *Кк* | k in **k**it |
| Лл | *Лл* | l in **l**ove |
| Мм | *Мм* | m in **m**ay |
| Нн | *Нн* | n in **n**ot |
| Оо | *Оо* | o in t**o**p |
| Пп | *Пп* | p in **p**ot |
| Рр | *Рр* | r in **r**ot (rolled) |
| Сс | *Сс* | s in **s**et |
| Тт | *Тт* | t in **t**o |
| Уу | *Уу* | oo in m**oo**n |
| Фф | *Фф* | f in **f**it |
| Хх | *Хх* | ch in lo**ch** (Scottish) |
| Цц | *Цц* | ts in ve**ts** |
| Чч | *Чч* | ch in **ch**in |
| Шш | *Шш* | sh in **sh**in |
| Щщ | *Щщ* | shch in pu**shch**air |
| ъ | *ъ* | hard sign (see page 36) |
| ы | *ы* | y in ph**y**sics |
| ь | *ь* | soft sign (see page 28) |
| Ээ | *Ээ* | e in m**e**t |
| Юю | *Юю* | yu in **Yu**le |
| Яя | *Яя* | ya in **ya**p |

# Здрáвствуйте!

- saying hello, goodbye
    . . . and how are you?
- introducing yourself
    . . . and asking someone's name

**В Россúи . . .** (In Russia . . . )
(Pronounced *v Rassee'ee*)

how you address someone will depend on how well
you know them. You use formal language to talk to a
waiter, receptionist or shop assistant or someone you
don't know well, and informal language to a friend, a
child or someone you know very well. Russians use a
middle name formed from their father's first name:
Pavel and Anna, whose father's name is Ivan, are called
**Pavel Ivanovich** and **Anna Ivanovna**. Short forms
of first names are common: **Вáня**, *Vanya* is the
common short form for **Ивáн**, *Eevan* and **Óля**, *Olya*
for **Óльга**, *Olga*.

# Saying hello, goodbye . . .

1   Listen to these key phrases.

**Здра́вствуйте**          Hello (formal)
Zdrastvooytye

**Здра́вствуй**           Hello (informal)
Zdrastvooy

**До свида́ния**          Goodbye
Da sveedaneeya

**По-ру́сски . . .** (In Russian . . . )
*Pa-rooskee . . .*

use **Здра́вствуйте** to greet one person formally or more than one person.

2   Anna, a tourist guide, greets a new arrival at the hotel. Listen and tick the word she uses to say 'hello'.

**Здра́вствуй**                  **Здра́вствуйте**

3   Listen as Anna greets five more people in the hotel. How many of them are young people or children?

4   Some guests are arriving and some leaving. As you hear each person, tick whether they are saying hello or goodbye to Anna.

|  | 1 | 2 | 3 | 4 | 5 |
|---|---|---|---|---|---|
| **Здра́вствуйте** | ■ | ■ | ■ | ■ | ■ |
| **До свида́ния** | ■ | ■ | ■ | ■ | ■ |

# . . . and how are you?

**5**  Listen to these key phrases.

**Как у вас дела́?**  How are you? (formal)
Kak oo vas dyela?

**Спаси́бо, хорошо́**  Thank you, fine
Spaseeba, kharasho

**А как у вас?**  And you? (formal)
A kak oo vas?

**6**  Listen to Anna greeting one of the tourists. Write in English what she asks him.

Спаси́бо, хорошо́

**7**  Ivan asks Anna how she is, using **Как дела́?** *Kak dyela?* the informal way of asking someone how they are. Listen, and give her reply in English.

**8**  At a summer language school in Moscow, Olga is teaching her students to read. Pointing to phrases on the board, she reads them aloud. Listen and number the phrases 1 to 6, in the order in which she reads them.

**Здра́вствуй** ............  **Как у вас дела́?** ............
**А как у вас?** ............  **Здра́вствуйте** ............
**Спаси́бо, хорошо́** ............  **До свида́ния** ............

# Introducing yourself . . .

**1** Listen to these key phrases.

**Меня зовут . . .**　　　　My name is . . .
Menya zavoot

**Как вас зовут?**　　　　What's your name? (formal)
Kak vas zavoot?

**2** Staff at the Moscow language school are introducing themselves to students. Tick the four names you hear.

Svetlana ▨　　Irina ▨

Victor ▨　　Yuri ▨

Tanya ▨　　Olga ▨

Vladimir ▨　　Ivan ▨

**3** Listen to these key phrases.

**Óчень рад**　　　　Pleased to meet you (said by a man)
Ochen rad

**Óчень ра́да**　　　　Pleased to meet you (said by a woman)
Ochen rada

**Простите?**　　　　Pardon?/Excuse me?/Sorry?
Prasteetye

**4** Lisa, a student, doesn't quite catch her new teacher's name. Does she use **Простите?** or **Как вас зовут?** to ask him to repeat it? What is his name?

Why does Lisa say **Óчень ра́да**, 'pleased to meet you', in a different way from Victor, who says **Óчень рад?**

# ... and asking someone's name

5  **Áнна**, *Anna*, meets **Táня**, *Tanya*, whose name she has forgotten. She's with her younger brother **Борис**, *Barees*. Listen to the recording and write the letter of the missing word in the appropriate gap.

| | |
|---|---|
| Anna | **Здра́вствуйте.** |
| Tanya | ...........................**.** |
| Anna | **Как** ............. **зову́т?** |
| Tanya | **Меня́ зову́т Та́ня.** ............. **вас зову́т?** |
| Anna | ............. **зову́т А́нна, а как тебя́ зову́т?** |
| Boris | **Меня́ зову́т Бори́с.** |
| Anna | **О́чень ра́да.** |
| Boris | ............. **рад.** |

*a* **Как**
*b* **Здра́вствуйте**
*c* **О́чень**
*d* **вас**
*e* **Меня́**

## По-ру́сски ...

to ask a child or a young person their name, use the informal **Как тебя́ зову́т?** *Kak tebya zavoot?* instead of **Как вас зову́т?**

6  Olga asks her students to do some more reading practice. Listen and number the phrases 1 to 6 in the order in which she says them.

**Как вас зову́т?** .............  **Как дела́?** .............
**Как тебя́ зову́т?** .............  **О́чень рад** .............
**Меня́ зову́т А́нна** .............  **Прости́те?** .............

# Put it all together

**1** The alphabet is fun to learn and you can already recognize several letters. Concentrate now on the ones which are highlighted below.

**абвгде**ёж**зийклмно**прст**у**фх**ц**чшщъыьэюя

**2** Six letters sound very similar to the English letters they look like. Listen to the cassette to check your pronunciation.

**Аа** (a)   **Ее** (ye)   **Кк** (k)   **Мм** (m)   **Оо** (o)   **Тт** (t)

Can you now read and guess the meaning of the following words? The first two can be found in the key phrases, others in the glossary.

| | | | | | | | |
|---|---|---|---|---|---|---|---|
| *a* | **а** | *b* | **как** | *c* | **мáма** | *d* | **такт** |
| *e* | **áтом** | *f* | **кóма** | *g* | **атáка** | *h* | **комéта** |

**3** Another six letters look like English but sound different:

**Вв** (v)   **Нн** (n)   **Рр** (r)   **Сс** (s)   **Уу** (oo)   **Хх** (kh, or ch as in 'loch')

Now read and guess the meaning of the following:

| | | | | | | | |
|---|---|---|---|---|---|---|---|
| *a* | **метрó** | *b* | **теáтр** | *c* | **ресторáн** | *d* | **трáктор** |
| *e* | **курс** | *f* | **Москвá** | *g* | **оркéстр** | *h* | **харáктер** |

**4** Match the Russian with the English. Write the correct letter in front of the English phrase.

| | | |
|---|---|---|
| *a* | **До свидáния** | My name's Anna |
| *b* | **Как вас зовýт?** | Pleased to meet you |
| *c* | **Меня зовýт Áнна** | How are you? |
| *d* | **Óчень рад** | Goodbye |
| *e* | **Как у вас делá?** | What's your name? |

# "Now you're talking!

I  As you're leaving your hotel, you meet your tour guide.

◆ Say hello to her.
◇ **Здравствуйте. Как у вас дела?**
◆ Say you're well and ask how she is.
◇ **Спасибо, хорошо.**

Another guide joins her.
◆ Greet him and introduce yourself.
◇ **Óчень рад. Меня зовут Иван.**
◆ He spoke very fast. Ask him to repeat his name.
◇ **Меня зовут Иван.**
◆ The guides have to leave. Say goodbye to them.

2  You're at a newspaper kiosk.

◆ Greet the vendor.
◇ **Здравствуйте.**
◆ Say hello to his son . . .
◇ **Здравствуйте.**
◆ . . . and ask him what his name is.
◇ **Меня зовут Саша.**
◆ Now ask him how he is.
◇ **Спасибо, хорошо.**

3  Now try the following:

◆ greet the waiter in a restaurant
◆ ask him his name
◆ ask him how he is
◆ as you leave the restaurant, say goodbye to him.

## Quiz

1 Which of the following names is Anna?
  *a* **Ваня**    *b* **Таня**    *c* **Áнна**
2 Where in Russia would you be if you were were in **Москва**?
3 Who is Sasha calling: **'Мáма'**?
4 Where would you be if you were in a **рестора́н**?
5 To say hello to a child would you use:
  *a* **Здра́вствуйте** or *b* **Здра́вствуй**?
6 How well would you know a person to use **Как дела́**?
7 To say 'pleased to meet you' would a man use:
  *a* **Óчень рад** or *b* **Óчень ра́да**?
8 Which of the following means 'Goodbye'?
  *a* **Здра́вствуйте**    *b* **До свида́ния**    *c* **Прости́те**
9 When asking a child's name do you say:
  *a* **Как вас зову́т?** or *b* **Как тебя́ зову́т?**
10 Which of the following means 'Thank you'?
  *a* **Спаси́бо**    *b* **Cа́ша**    *c* **Хорошо́**

# Now check whether you can . . .

▣  greet someone you don't know well

▣  greet a child

▣  say goodbye

▣  ask someone's name and give your name

▣  ask how someone is and say how you are

▣  say 'Pardon?/Excuse me?/Sorry?'

Listen to the recordings as often as possible. Repeat the words and phrases before you look at them in the book. Then read them after the voices. Finally, try to read them without listening to the recordings. By doing this you should find that you will soon be reading Russian without any prompts.

# Я англичáнин

- asking someone's nationality
  . . . and stating yours
- saying whether you are married
- using the numbers 0 to 4

## В Росси́и . . .

people are friendly and hospitable. If you can ask a few simple questions and say a little about yourself, the Russians you meet will be delighted.

Remember that if you speak Russian you should also be understood in many of the new independent republics, e.g. **Гру́зия** *Groozeeya* (Georgia), **Украи́на** *Ookraeena* (Ukraine), **Белору́ссия** *Byelaroosseeya* (Belarus).

# Asking someone's nationality . . .

| Listen to these key phrases.

**Вы / Ты . . .**
Vy / ty . . .

**. . . англича́нин / англича́нка?**
angleechaneen / angleechanka?

**Да, я . . .**
Da, ya . . .

**Нет, я не . . .**
Nyet, ya nye . . .

**. . . англича́нин / англича́нка**

Are you (formal / informal) . . .

. . . English (m. / f.)?

Yes, I am . . .

No, I'm not . . .

. . . English (m. / f.)

---

**По-ру́сски . . .**

there are no words for 'am, is, are'. You simply say **я** (I) for 'I am' and **вы / ты** (you) for 'you are'.

---

2 Listen as Olga asks four summer school students (**студе́нты**, *stoodyenty*) about themselves. Tick which nationality each of them is:

|       | English | American | Australian | Canadian |
|-------|---------|----------|------------|----------|
| David | ■       | ■        | ■          | ■        |
| Ann   | ■       | ■        | ■          | ■        |
| Lisa  | ■       | ■        | ■          | ■        |
| Mark  | ■       | ■        | ■          | ■        |

---

**По-ру́сски . . .**

there are no words for 'the' or 'a', but Russians do distinguish between masculine and feminine. The key is in the word ending.

Many masculine words end in a consonant (**англича́нин, студе́нт**), while many feminine words end in **-а** (**англича́нка, студе́нтка**).

---

# . . . and stating yours

**3** Listen to the recording and repeat the following countries.

Can you match the English with the Russian?

| | | |
|---|---|---|
| a | **Аме́рика** | Russia |
| b | **Кана́да** | Britain |
| c | **А́нглия** | Australia |
| d | **Росси́я** | England |
| e | **Брита́ния** | America |
| f | **Австра́лия** | Canada |

**4** Now match the letter of the country above to the corresponding nationality below. How many are women?

| | | | |
|---|---|---|---|
| 1 | **Я ру́сский**<br>Ya roosskeey | 4 | **Я америка́нка**<br>Ya amereekanka |
| 2 | **Я англича́нка**<br>Ya angleechanka | 5 | **Я австрали́ец**<br>Ya avstraleeyets |
| 3 | **Я кана́дец**<br>Ya kanadets | 6 | **Я брита́нец**<br>Ya breetanets |

## По-ру́сски . . .

**он**, *on*, (he) means 'he is' and **она́**, *ana*, (she) means 'she is'.

**5** Olga has written down the nationality of some of her students and fellow teachers. Give their nationality in English. Are they men or women?

| | nationality | | male | female |
|---|---|---|---|---|
| a | **Он англича́нин** | ............................... | ■ | ■ |
| b | **Она́ америка́нка** | ............................... | ■ | ■ |
| c | **Он ру́сский** | ............................... | ■ | ■ |
| d | **Он кана́дец** | ............................... | ■ | ■ |

# Saying whether you are married

1 Listen to these key phrases.

| | |
|---|---|
| **Вы / Ты . . .** | Are you . . . |
| **. . . жена́ты / жена́т?**<br>zhenaty / zhenat? | . . . married? (formal / informal, said to a man) |
| **. . . за́мужем?**<br>zamoozhem? | . . . married? (formal / informal, said to a woman) |
| **Да, я жена́т / за́мужем** | Yes, I am married (m. / f.) |
| **Нет, я не жена́т / за́мужем** | No, I am not married (m. / f.) |

2 Listen, and tick which students tell Olga they are married.

**Дави́д** ■     **Анн** ■     **Ли́са** ■     **Марк** ■
David         Ann         Lisa         Mark

3 Listen to Olga introducing herself to her students, and tick the statements which are true. Listen out for the word **москви́чка** (*maskveechka*), which means a woman from Moscow.

a Her name is Olga Sergeyevna
b Her father's name is Ivan
c She is Russian
d She is married

4 She now asks her students to introduce themselves in the same way. Complete the register for her in English.

| Name | Nationality | Marital status |
|---|---|---|
| a | | |
| b | | |
| c | | |
| d | | |

# Using the numbers 0 to 4

**1** Listen to the following numbers.

| 0 | 1 | 2 | 3 | 4 |
|---|---|---|---|---|
| **ноль** | **один** | **два** | **три** | **четыре** |
| nol | adeen | dva | tree | chetyre |

**2** Olga is teaching her summer class these numbers. Enter the figures 0 to 4 as you hear them.

a ...........................................
b ...........................................
c ...........................................
d ...........................................
e ...........................................

**3** She gives them a few simple sums. Put in the missing figure as in the example.

a **один +   2   = три**
b **четыре - _____ = один**
c **_____ + один = два**
d **один + три = _____**

**4** Olga wants her class to do some more reading practice. Listen as she reads the following and write the numbers 1 to 8 in the order in which she reads them from the board.

| | | | |
|---|---|---|---|
| **Вы англичанин?** | ■ | **Да, он англичанин** | ■ |
| **Вы замужем?** | ■ | **Она не американка** | ■ |
| **Ты женат?** | ■ | **Она замужем** | ■ |
| **Она москвичка** | ■ | **Вы женаты?** | ■ |

# Put it all together

1 Focus on the highlighted letters below:

а**б**в**гд**е**ё**ж**зи**й**кл**мнопрстуф**хц**ч**шщъ**ы**ьэю**я**

2 **Гг** (g)    **Жж** (zh)    **Зз** (z)    **Ии** (ee)

**Жж** sounds like 's' in 'pleasure'.

So read and guess the meaning of the following words:

*a*  **газ**    *b*  **газéта**    *c*  **жест**    *d*  **таксú**

3 **Лл** (l)    **Чч** (ch)    **ы** (y)    **Яя** (ya)

**ы** sounds roughly like 'y' in 'physics'. It can never begin a word.

So read and guess the following:

*a*  **литр**    *b*  **матч**    *c*  **вы**    *d*  **я**

4 See how many of these words you already know or can guess:

*a*  **вúски**    *b*  **килогрáмм**  *c*  **Чéхов**    *d*  **киóск**
*e*  **туалéт**    *f*  **винó**    *g*  **москвúч**    *h*  **москвúчка**

5 Match the Russian with the English. Write the correct letters in the boxes.

*a*  **Онá зáмужем**        ░░  He's a student
*b*  **Он женáт**        ░░  I'm not English (m.)
*c*  **Онá студéнтка**        ░░  She's married
*d*  **Он студéнт**        ░░  He's married
*e*  **Я не англичáнин**        ░░  She's a student

# Now you're talking!

**I** Imagine you're Maria Foster, an English student at a Moscow summer school, where you are introducing yourself to the teacher.

- ◆ Greet him.
- ◇ **Здра́вствуйте. Как вас зову́т?**
- ◆ Answer his question and find out his name.
- ◇ **Меня́ зову́т Ива́н. Как у вас дела́?**
- ◆ Say you're fine and ask if he's a Muscovite.
- ◇ **Да, я москви́ч.**
- ◆ Give your nationality.
- ◇ **О́чень рад.**
- ◆ Reply appropriately.

**2** Now imagine you're Ross Smart. Give your details to the teacher.

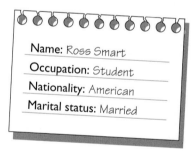

Name: Ross Smart
Occupation: Student
Nationality: American
Marital status: Married

**3** Later, in the dining room, you start talking to the man sitting next to you. How would you ask him if he's:

- ◆ Russian?
- ◆ a Muscovite?
- ◆ a student?
- ◆ married?

# Quiz

1  Would an American woman say:
   a **Я американец?** or b **Я американка?**
2  If a man said **Я британец**, where would he be from?
3  Put the numbers in the right order:
   a **три**  b **один**  c **четыре**  d **два**
4  Which country would you be from if you lived in **Канада**?
5  What is the difference in meaning between a **да** and b **нет**?
6  Which word would you insert into the middle of **Я русский** to say
   'I'm not Russian'?
   a **он**  b **она**  c **не**
7  Which of the following is not a drink?
   a **виски**  b **киоск**  c **вино**
8  If a woman tells you she is **москвичка**, where is she from?
9  Who is married – Ivan or Anna? **Иван не женат, а Анна
   замужем.**
10  Name this famous writer: **Чехов**.

# Now check whether you can . . .

- ■ say yes and no

- ■ say what nationality you are

- ■ say whether you are married or not

- ■ ask others for this information

- ■ use the numbers 0 to 4

Concentrate for now on understanding and reading Russian. Listen to
the recordings frequently. As you don't yet know how to write
Russian, to help you learn new words and phrases you could try
recording yourself speak. Don't try to copy the printed version from
the book, since Russian has a different handwritten form (see page 6).

# Это Анна

- **introducing friends**

  **. . . and members of your family**
- **talking about your family**
- **giving your phone number**
- **using the numbers 5 to 10**

## В России . . .

families nowadays tend to be small, generally with one or two children. The **бабушка**, *babooshka* (grandmother), still plays an important role in looking after the children while the mother works. However, recently there has been a tendency towards mothers staying at home when the children are very young.

# Introducing friends . . .

1  Listen to these key phrases.

| | |
|---|---|
| **Это Áнна**<br>Eta Anna | This is Anna |
| **Это мой друг**<br>Eta moy droog | This is my friend (m.) |
| **Это моя подрýга**<br>Eta maya padrooga | This is my friend (f.) |
| **Это мой муж**<br>Eta moy moozh | This is my husband |
| **Это моя женá**<br>Eta maya zhena | This is my wife |

2  Olga, the summer school teacher, introduces two of her colleagues to
David, a student. Can you work out where each name belongs in the
dialogue? Write the letter of the missing name in the gap.

| | |
|---|---|
| Olga | **Это моя подрýга** ................... |
| David | **Óчень рад.** |
| Olga | **Это мой друг** ................... |
| David | **Óчень рад.** |

*a* **Лéна** (Lyena, a woman's name)   *b* **Лев** (Lyev, a man's name)

**По-рýсски** . . .

the word for 'my' is
   **мой** for masculine words, e.g. **мой муж**
   **моя** for feminine words, e.g. **моя женá**

3  Listen to Lyena and Lyev introducing their partners to David.
Tick the correct name.

Lyena's husband is:  **Вйктор** (Victor)   **Владймир** (Vladimir)
Lyev's wife is:  **Лáра** (Lara)   **Лйдия** (Lydia)

# ... and members of your family

**4** Listen to these key phrases.

| | |
|---|---|
| **У вас есть дети?**<br>Oo vas yest dyetee? | Do you have children? |
| **Да, у меня есть ...**<br>Da, oo menya yest ... | Yes, I have ... |
| **... сын**<br>... syn | ... a son |
| **и ...**<br>ee ... | and ... |
| **... дочь**<br>... doch | ... a daughter |
| **Как его / её зовут?**<br>Kak ye_vo / yeyo zavoot? | What is he / she called? |
| **Его / Её зовут ...**<br>Ye_vo / Yeyo zavoot ... | He / She is called ... |

Sometimes, as here, **г** is pronounced v.

**5** Listen as David asks if Lyena and Lyev have any children. Tick the statements which are true **да** (yes) or false **нет** (no).

| | | да | нет |
|---|---|:---:|:---:|
| *a* | Lyena has a son | ■ | ■ |
| *b* | Lyev has a son | ■ | ■ |

**6** David asks Olga the names of two other friends. Listen and tick the correct name.

The woman's name is:    **Наташа** (Natasha)    **Нина** (Nina)
The man's name is:    **Пётр** (Pyotr)    **Павел** (Pavel)

# Talking about your family

**1**  Listen to these key phrases.

**Э́то . . .**
Eta . . .

Is this . . .

**. . . ваш / твой брат?**
. . . vash / tvoy brat?

. . . your brother? (formal / informal)

**. . . ва́ша / твоя́ сестра́?**
. . . vasha / tvaya sestra?

. . . your sister? (formal / informal)

**2**  Nina and Pavel tell David about their families. Tick the statements which are true.

a   Nina has one sister      b   Pavel has a daughter
c   Nina has two brothers    d   Pavel is not married

**3**  Vera describes her family tree. Write the letters of the missing words in the gaps. Look up any new words in the glossary.

| | |
|---|---|
| a | за́мужем |
| b | муж |
| c | ба́бушка |
| d | дочь |
| e | Никола́й |
| f | жена́т |

**Меня́ зову́т Ве́ра. Я за́мужем. Э́то мой** ............... **Его́
зову́т Серге́й. У меня́ есть сын. Его́ зову́т** ...............
**Он не** ............... **У меня́ та́кже есть** ............... **Её зову́т
Ири́на. Она́** ............... **У неё есть дочь, ита́к я** ............... **.**

**По-ру́сски . . .**

**У неё / него́ есть** means 'she / he has'.
To ease pronunciation **н** is sometimes added to **её** and **его́**.

# Giving your phone number

I   Listen to the following numbers.

| 5 | 6 | 7 | 8 | 9 | 10 |
|---|---|---|---|---|---|
| **пять** | **шесть** | **семь** | **восемь** | **девять** | **десять** |
| pyat | shyest | syem | vosem | dyevat | dyesat |

2   Olga is teaching her students some more numbers. Enter 5 to 10 in the order in which you hear them.

*a* ..............................     *b* ..............................

*c* ..............................     *d* ..............................

*e* ..............................     *f* ..............................

3   David and Mark give Olga their **номер телефона**, *nomer telefona* (telephone number) while resident in Moscow. Listen and make a note of them.

David ..............................
Mark ..............................

4   The code for Russia is 007, for Moscow 095 and for St Petersburg 812. Say the following two phone numbers out loud, giving the full code, then listen to the cassette to check your answers.

| Moscow | 6107252 |
|---|---|
| St Petersburg | 3961248 |

5   Olga gives her students some more reading practice. Listen, and note the order, 1 to 6, of what she reads.

**Это моя подруга** ..........     **Это мой муж** ..........

**У вас есть дети?** ..........     **Это твой брат?** ..........

**Как его зовут?** ..........     **У неё есть сын** ..........

# Put it all together

**1** Focus on the highlighted letters below:

а**бвгд**е**ёж**зи**й**клмно**прст**уфх**ц**чшщъыь**э**юя**

**2** **Бб** (b)    **Дд** (d)    **Ёё** (yo)    **Йй** (y)    **Пп** (p)    **Ээ** (e)

**Ёё** sounds like 'yo' in 'your'.
**й** is used mainly after vowels. It sounds like 'y' in boy.

Read and guess the meaning of the following words:

| | | |
|---|---|---|
| *a* **бар** | *b* **дáма** | *c* **еë** |
| *d* **мой** | *e* **парк** | *f* **экзáмен** |

**3** The letter **ь** has no sound of its own. It softens the letter before it and is known as a soft sign.

Both masculine and feminine words can end in **ь**.

Guess the meaning of: **автомобúль** (m.)

**4** Now see how many of these words you can guess:

| | | |
|---|---|---|
| *a* **диплóм** | *b* **автóбус** | *c* **Толстóй** |
| *d* **экспéрт** | *e* **университéт** | *f* **трамвáй** |

**5** Match the Russian with the English. Write the correct letter in front of the English phrase.

| | | |
|---|---|---|
| *a* | **Это Вúктор** | I also have a son |
| *b* | **Это вáша женá?** | This is Victor |
| *c* | **У меня тáкже есть сын** | Have you any children? |
| *d* | **У негó есть сын** | What's her name? |
| *e* | **Как её зовут?** | He has a son |
| *f* | **У вас есть дéти?** | Is this your wife? |

# Now you're talking!

**1** Imagine you're Ben Carter and the teacher at the summer school is asking you about your family. You show her the photograph below.

- ◆ Tell her you are married.
- ◇ **Это ваша жена?**
- ◆ Say yes and give her name.
- ◇ **У вас есть дети?**
- ◆ Say you have a son and give his name.
- ◇ **Он женат?**
- ◆ Explain that he's not married but he has a daughter.
- ◇ **А . . . , хорошо.**

**2** Now imagine you are Lisa Parker. Give your details to the teacher.

| | |
|---|---|
| Name: | Lisa Parker |
| Occupation: | Student |
| Nationality: | English |
| Marital status: | Married |
| No. of children: | A daughter |
| Child's name: | Vanessa |

# Quiz

1   To say 'my sister' would you use *a* **мой** or *b* **моя** in front of **сестра́**?

2   If someone asked: **Это твой брат?** would they be using the formal or informal 'your'?

3   Put the numbers in the right order:
    *a* **семь**   *b* **де́сять**   *c* **шесть**   *d* **во́семь**   *e* **пять**   *f* **де́вять**

4   What would you be giving someone if you gave them your **но́мер телефо́на?**

5   Which is the odd one out?
    *a* **авто́бус**   *b* **парк**   *c* **трамва́й**

6   Name this famous writer: **Толсто́й**.

7   What does **та́кже** mean?

8   If you said: **Это моя́ подру́га** would you be introducing a male or female friend?

# Now check whether you can . . .

■  introduce someone – male or female

■  talk simply about your family / friends

■  ask others for similar information

■  give your phone number and use the numbers 5 to 10

---

A good way to practise introducing people is to use a family photograph. Point to each person and say who they are:

e.g. **Это мой брат Дави́д**    **Это моя́ сестра́ А́нна**

The following words might come in useful:

| | |
|---|---|
| **ма́ма / мать** (mama / mat) | mum / mother |
| **па́па / оте́ц** (papa / atyets) | dad / father |
| **де́душка** (dyedooshka) | grandfather |
| **тётя** (tyotya), **дя́дя** (dyadya) | aunt, uncle |

# 4

# Чай, пожа́луйста

- ● ordering a drink in a bar or café
- ● offering, accepting or refusing a drink
- ● using the numbers 11 to 20

## В Росси́и . . .

you can get a drink or snack in a **бар** (bar) or **кафе́** (café), although it can be rather expensive. The **бар** is open until late at night and often has music and dancing. You place your order with the **бармен** (barman), but the **кафе́** can be self-service.

In the street you will find a **кио́ск** (kiosk) where you can buy **моро́женое**, *marozhenoye* (ice cream), which is very popular even in the sub-zero temperatures of winter.

# Ordering a drink . . .

**1**  Listen to these key phrases.

**Что вам угодно?**
Shto vam oogodna?

What would you like?

**Чай, пожáлуйста**
Chay, pazhalsta

Tea, please

**Кóфе, пожáлуйста**
Kofye

Coffee, please

**Хорошó**
**Спасúбо**
**Пожáлуйста**

OK, that's fine
Thank you
You're welcome

**2**  Anna orders a drink in the hotel. Listen and decide whether she orders tea or coffee.

**3**  The family next to her orders four different drinks. Who has what?

|  | **водá**<br>vada<br>(water) | **винó**<br>veeno<br>(wine) | **пúво**<br>peeva<br>(beer) | **лимонáд**<br>leemonad<br>(lemonade) |
|---|---|---|---|---|
| **пáпа** |  |  |  |  |
| **мáма** |  |  |  |  |
| **сын** |  |  |  |  |
| **дочь** |  |  |  |  |

## По-рýсски . . .

all nouns are masculine (m.), feminine (f.) or neuter (n.).
Masculine nouns usually end in a **consonant** or **й**: **лимонáд**, **чай**
Feminine nouns usually end in **-a** or **-я**: **водá**, **тётя**
Neuter nouns usually end in **-o** or **-e**: **винó**, **морóженое**

As there is no word for 'the' or 'a', **чай** can mean 'tea', 'a tea' or 'the tea'.

# . . . in a bar or café

**4**   Listen as other people arrive and order drinks.

What does the man order?

Does the woman have her coffee **с сáхаром**, s sakharom (with sugar) or **без сáхара**, byez sakhara (without sugar)?

**5**   How does Tanya order her coffee? Does she want any sugar?

*a*   with milk (**с молокóм**, s malakom)
*b*   without milk (**без молокá**, byez malaka)

**6**   Listen as Ivan orders tea, and decide whether he wants it with sugar, milk or lemon.

**7**   Does Victor order sparkling (**с гáзом**, s gazom) or still (**без гáза**, byez gaza) mineral water?

**8**   How would you ask for:

- a beer?
- a coffee with milk?
- tea without sugar?

# Offering, accepting or refusing a drink

1   Listen to these key phrases.

| | |
|---|---|
| **Что вы хотите?**<br>Shto vy khateetye? | What would you like (formal)? |
| **Что ты хочешь?**<br>Shto ty khochyesh? | What would you like (informal)? |
| **. . . а вы / ты?** | . . . and for you (formal / informal)? |
| **Да, пожалуйста** | Yes, please |
| **Нет, спасибо** | No, thank you |

2   Anna is in the hotel bar. Listen as she offers one of the visitors a drink.

What does he ask for?

When he thanks her, which of the following words does Anna use to say 'You're welcome'?

*a* **Хорошо**    *b* **Пожалуйста**    *c* **Спасибо**

3   Katya and Misha, two of Anna's colleagues, come into the bar, so she offers them a drink too. Katya wants a fruit juice (**сок**, *sok*). What does Misha order? Which phrase does Anna use to Katya and why?

*a* **Что вы хотите?**    *b* **Что ты хочешь?**

## По-русски . . .

**вы** (you) is used to address more than one person, as well as one person in a formal situation.

Sometimes the word for 'you' is left out altogether:
**Что хочешь?** (What would you like?)

# Using the numbers 11 to 20

1 Olga has taken her summer school class out for the day. Ten of the students have already set off with two other teachers. Listen as she does a head count of the others.

| | | | |
|---|---|---|---|
| 11 | одиннадцать | 16 | шестнадцать |
| 12 | двенадцать | 17 | семнадцать |
| 13 | тринадцать | 18 | восемнадцать |
| 14 | четырнадцать | 19 | девятнадцать |
| 15 | пятнадцать | 20 | двадцать |

2 They all go into a café and Olga has to order for everyone. Listen to her order and fill in the number of drinks and ice creams ordered:

Лимонад ........................

Пепси-кола ........................

Мороженое ........................

3 Back in class Olga gives her students some number practice. Write down in the spaces the numbers that you hear.

*a* ............ *b* ............ *c* ............ *d* ............ *e* ............

4 She also asks them to put the following dialogue in the correct order. Can you? Number the phrases one to five appropriately.

Коньяк, пожалуйста.

Что ты хочешь?

Пожалуйста.

Коньяк? Хорошо.

Спасибо.

# Put it all together

**1**  Once you've studied the following highlighted letters, you'll have reached the end of the Russian alphabet! **Бра́во!** Well done!

абвгдеёжзийклмнопрсту**фхцчшщъ**ыьэюя

**2**  **Фф** (f)  **Цц** (ts)  **Шш** (sh)  **Щщ** (shch)  **Юю** (yu)

**Цц** sounds like 'ts' in 'pets'
**Щщ** sounds like 'shch' in 'pushchair'

So read and guess the meaning of the following words:

*a* **фа́нта**  *b* **центр**  *c* **шампа́нское**  *d* **борщ**  *e* **меню́**

**3**  Like the soft sign **ь**, the hard sign **ъ** has no sound of its own, and is rarely used. Between a consonant and a vowel, it can indicate a slight pause between the two sounds. Listen to the pronunciation of **съезд**, which means 'congress', and **объе́кт**, which you can probably guess. If not you'll find the answer on page 105.

**4**  You now have the Russian alphabet under your belt, so have some fun reading and translating the following:

*a* **администра́тор**  *b* **телефо́н**  *c* **конце́рт**
*d* **Чайко́вский**  *e* **Росси́я**  *f* **Санкт-Петербу́рг**

**5**  Match the Russian with the English. Write the correct letter in front of the English phrase.

| | | |
|---|---|---|
| *a* | **Пи́во, пожа́луйста** | Coffee without sugar |
| *b* | **Что вам уго́дно?** | Tea with milk |
| *c* | **Чай с молоко́м** | You're welcome |
| *d* | **Ко́фе без са́хара** | A beer, please |
| *e* | **Пожа́луйста** | What would you like? |

# "Now you're talking!

I  You're attending a conference in St Petersburg with Andrey, a Russian business colleague, whom you've got to know very well.

♦ In the bar you ask him what he'd like to drink.
◇ **Пи́во, пожа́луйста.**
♦ As you are about to order, his wife, whom you've only met once before, joins you both. Ask her what she'd like.
◇ **Пе́пси-ко́ла, пожа́луйста.**
♦ Now greet the barman and order a beer, a coke and a lemonade.

2  Now imagine you're in a café in Novgorod.

♦ Greet the waitress.
◇ **Здра́вствуйте. Что вам уго́дно?**
♦ Order a tea.
◇ **С са́харом?**
♦ Say with sugar but no milk.
◇ **Хорошо́.**
♦ When the drink arrives, thank the waitress.
◇ **Пожа́луйста.**

3  Try the following:

♦ ask your good friend Igor if he wants a coffee
♦ ask if he wants the coffee with sugar
♦ check if he wants it with milk
♦ finally, order his coffee with milk but no sugar.

## Quiz

1 Which is the odd one out?
   *a* **са́хар**   *b* **молоко́**   *c* **чай**   *d* **ко́фе**
2 Which alcoholic drink would you get if you ordered **коньяк**?
3 Put the numbers in the right order:
   *a* **восемна́дцать**   *b* **семна́дцать**   *c* **девятна́дцать**
4 Give the three English meanings of **ко́фе**.
5 Are nouns ending in **-о** m., f. or n.?
6 What would you get with your tea if you ordered **чай с лимо́ном**?
7 What would you get if you ordered **моро́женое**?
8 If you asked for **минера́льная вода́ без га́за** would you get still or sparkling mineral water?
9 Who is the **барме́н**?

# Now check whether you can . . .

■ order a drink in a bar / café

■ offer someone a drink

■ accept or refuse politely when someone offers you a drink

■ say whether you want your drink with or without something

■ use the numbers 11 to 20

Now that you've completed the alphabet, go back to the beginning of the book and read all the Russian words and phrases you've met so far. Check your pronunciation with the recordings.

Don't worry at this stage about making mistakes or about words changing their endings, e.g. **са́хар / с са́харом**. If you know the basic word you'll be able to make yourself understood. As you gain confidence, you'll find it easier to focus on the detail.

# Контро́льная рабо́та 1

**1** Olga is interviewing one of her summer school students.
Listen, and tick the details that match what he tells her.

| | | | |
|---|---|---|---|
| **Ро́бин Мо́рсон** | **англича́нин** ☐ | **австрали́ец** ☐ |
| **Он** | **жена́т** ☐ | **не жена́т** ☐ |
| **У него́ есть** | **сын** ☐ | **дочь** ☐ |
| **Его́ зову́т** | **Кри́стиан** ☐ | **Кри́стофер** ☐ |

**2** David, one of the students, has become friendly with a Russian
student, Anton, who has invited him to his flat in Moscow. Listen,
then fill in the missing details in English.

David meets Anton's ........................ and ........................ .

Anton's sister's name is ........................ .

She says she is ................................................ .

David is from ................................................ .

**3** Listen as Anton offers David a drink. Tick the drink he is *not* offered.

*a* **пи́во**   *b* **вино́**   *c* **лимона́д**   *d* **ко́фе**   *e* **чай**

**4** Read the names of these drinks aloud, then check your pronunciation
with the cassette. Look up the meaning of any you don't understand in
the glossary.

| | | | | |
|---|---|---|---|---|
| во́дка | конья́к | фа́нта | чай | тома́тный сок |
| лимона́д | вино́ | джин | ко́фе | шампа́нское |
| ви́ски | ром | молоко́ | вода́ | пе́пси-ко́ла |

**5** From your study of the alphabet you'll have noticed that words of more than one syllable have a stress mark, which in turn affects the pronunciation of the other vowels. See if you can read and understand the names of these countries. Then check your pronunciation with the cassette, paying particular attention to how the word is stressed. Look up any words you're unsure of in the glossary.

| | | |
|---|---|---|
| Ирла́ндия | Уэ́льс | Шотла́ндия |
| Ита́лия | Испа́ния | Фра́нция |
| Гре́ция | Болга́рия | Герма́ния |

**6** Link the questions to the answers, e.g. *1 h.*

1 Как вас зову́т?
2 Вы англича́нка?
3 Вы за́мужем?
4 У вас есть де́ти?
5 Как его́ зову́т?
6 Как у вас дела́?
7 Что вам уго́дно?
8 Вы хоти́те ко́фе?

  *a* Да, я за́мужем.
  *b* Его́ зову́т Ива́н.
  *c* Да, пожа́луйста, с са́харом.
  *d* Спаси́бо, хорошо́.
  *e* Чай, пожа́луйста.
  *f* Да, у меня́ есть сын.
  *g* Нет, я ру́сская.
  *h* Меня́ зову́т Ири́на.

**7** Add the following numbers and write the answer in figures.

| | | |
|---|---|---|
| *a* | шестна́дцать + трина́дцать | = |
| *b* | четы́рнадцать + пять | = |
| *c* | семь + восемна́дцать | = |
| *d* | два́дцать + оди́ннадцать | = |
| *e* | двена́дцать + девятна́дцать | = |

**8** Choose the expression that fits each context.

1 In reply to **Как дела?**
2 The opposite of **Нет**.
3 You haven't heard something properly.
4 In reply to **Спасибо**.
5 Saying 'Goodbye'.
6 You're introduced to someone.

a  Простите?

b  До свидания

c  Очень рад

d  Да

e  Спасибо, хорошо

f  Пожалуйста

**9** Write the letter of the missing word in the appropriate gap.

1 **Это Бен. Он** .....................    a   **Иван**
2 **У** ............ **есть сестра..**    b   **американка**
3 ............ **зовут Ольга.**    c   **англичанин**
4 **Очень** ............    d   **меня**
5 **Меня зовут** ............    e   **рад**
6 ............ **у вас дела?**    f   **Её**
7 **Это Никола. Она** ............    g   **Как**

Take the first letter of each missing Russian word to find the name of a country.

**10** Elizabeth, a friend's daughter, has received the following letter from a Russian pen friend. The letter is typed but Masha has handwritten the beginning and her name. Can you translate it for Elizabeth? Any words you're unsure of can be found in the glossary.

*Дорогая Элизабет*

Меня зовут Máша. Я москвичка. Я студентка в Москве. Мой пáпа инженéр и моя мáма гид. У меня есть сестрá. Её зовýт Натáша. Онá шкóльница. У меня тáкже есть бáбушка. Мой нóмер телефóна: 007 095 1670355. До свидáния.

*Máша*

| | |
|---|---|
| **дорогáя** (f.) | dear |
| **инженéр** | engineer |
| **гид** | guide |
| **шкóльница** | schoolgirl |
| **в** | in |
| **и** | and |

You should be very proud of how much Russian you can read, understand and speak already. Don't try to write Russian yet – if you compare the printed and handwritten words from Elizabeth's letter, you will see that some letters look very different.

| **Дорогáя Элúзабет** | *Дорогая Элизабет* |
|---|---|
| **Máша** | *Máша* |

# Скажите, пожалуйста, где гостиница?

- asking where something is

  . . . and how far it is
- asking where someone lives
- using the numbers 21 to 199

**В России . . .**

many of the towns are rich in history, with beautiful squares, boulevards and interesting buildings. If you visit a **музей** (museum) you will find it packed with foreign and Russian tourists alike. **В Москве** (in Moscow) be sure to go to the **Кремль** (Kremlin), while **в Санкт-Петербурге** (in St Petersburg) no trip would be complete without a visit to the **Эрмитаж** (Hermitage Museum).

# Asking where something is . . .

1    Listen to these key phrases.

| | |
|---|---|
| **Прости́те, пожа́луйста** | Excuse me, please |
| **Скажи́те, пожа́луйста** | Tell me, please |
| **Где?** | Where? |
| **Где гости́ница?** | Where is the hotel? |
| **Где рестора́ны?** | Where are the restaurants? |
| **Иди́те . . .** | Go . . . |

**. . . пря́мо**

**. . . нале́во**                                          **. . . напра́во**

2    Listen as Lisa asks Olga where the following places are. Say where she wants to go in English, and tick the direction she should take.

| | | left | straight on | right |
|---|---|---|---|---|
| *a* | **по́чта** | | | |
| *b* | **метро́** | | | |
| *c* | **теа́тр** | | | |
| *d* | **гости́ница** | | | |
| *e* | **рестора́н** | | | |
| *f* | **музе́й** | | | |

## По-ру́сски . . .

nouns change their endings for the plural. There are a variety of endings which you will need to learn at a later stage. One of the most common endings is: **ы**

| | |
|---|---|
| **'Где гости́ницы?'** | Where are the hotels? |
| **'Где рестора́ны?'** | Where are the restaurants? |

# . . . and how far it is

**3**  Listen to these key phrases.

| | |
|---|---|
| **Это далеко?** | Is it far? |
| **Да, далеко** | Yes, it's a long way |
| **Нет, недалеко** | No, it's not far |
| **Десять минут пешком** | Ten minutes on foot |
| **Пять минут автобусом** | Five minutes by bus |
| **Один километр** | One kilometre |

**4**  Lisa now asks Olga if the places are far away. Listen and fill in the distance. Then tick whether she is told to go by bus or on foot.

| | | | on foot | by bus |
|---|---|---|---|---|
| a | The theatre is ............... minutes | | ▓▓ | ▓▓ |
| b | The museum is ............... minutes | | ▓▓ | ▓▓ |
| c | The post office is ............ minutes | | ▓▓ | ▓▓ |
| d | The hotel is .................. minutes | | ▓▓ | ▓▓ |
| e | The restaurant is ........... minutes | | ▓▓ | ▓▓ |
| f | The underground is ........ minutes | | ▓▓ | ▓▓ |

## По-русски . . .

the words for 'one' are **один** (m.) **одна** (f.) **одно** (n.)
**Два** (two) only has two forms: **два** (m., n.) and **две** (f.)

From two onwards, nouns change their endings after numbers:

| masculine | feminine | neuter |
|---|---|---|
| **один километр** | **одна минута** | **одно место** (place) |
| **два километра** | **две минуты** | **два места** |
| **пять километров** | **пять минут** | **пять мест** |

These rules take time to get used to – for the moment, just concentrate on understanding the number and the noun.

# Asking where someone lives

1  Listen to these key phrases.

| | |
|---|---|
| **Где вы живёте?** | Where do you live (formal)? |
| **Где ты живёшь?** | Where do you live (informal)? |
| **Я живу́ . . .** | I live . . . |
| **. . . в Санкт-Петербу́рге** | . . . in St Petersburg |
| **. . . в Но́вгороде** | . . . in Novgorod |
| **. . . в Волгогра́де** | . . . in Volgograd |

2  Listen to Olga asking some of her students where they live. Write down their home town in English.

Lisa     .................................................................

David   .................................................................

Mark   .................................................................

Ann     .................................................................

3  Olga asks two colleagues to tell her class if they live in Moscow. Listen, and write their replies in English, then tick the name of the colleague she knows quite well.

**Лев**    .................................................................

**Пётр**   .................................................................

---

**По-ру́сски . . .**

after **в** (in) nouns usually change their ending to **-е** (sometimes to **-и**):

| | |
|---|---|
| **Петербу́рг** | **в Петербу́рге** (in (St) Petersburg) |
| **Москва́** | **в Москве́** (in Moscow) |
| **Росси́я** | **в Росси́и** (in Russia) |

Some don't change at all, e.g. **в метро́** (in the underground).

# Using the numbers 21 to 199

1   Listen to the following numbers.

| | | | |
|---|---|---|---|
| 21 | два́дцать оди́н | 40 | со́рок |
| 22 | два́дцать два | 50 | пятьдеся́т |
| 23 | два́дцать три | 60 | шестьдеся́т |
| 24 | два́дцать четы́ре | 70 | се́мьдесят |
| 25 | два́дцать пять | 80 | во́семьдесят |
| 26 | два́дцать шесть | 90 | девяно́сто |
| 27 | два́дцать семь | 100 | сто |
| 28 | два́дцать во́семь | 101 | сто оди́н |
| 29 | два́дцать де́вять | 110 | сто де́сять |
| 30 | три́дцать | 142 | сто со́рок два |
| 31 | три́дцать оди́н, etc. | 199 | сто девяно́сто де́вять |

2   Olga shows her class the following envelope and reads it aloud.

She explains that **Куда́** indicates where the letter is going and **Кому́** tells us who it is being sent to.

Куда́:    г. Москва́

          ул. Тверска́я

          д. 15    кв. 52

Кому́:    Ивано́ву П. А.

> г. / го́род (town)
> ул. / у́лица (street)
> д. / дом (house/block)
> кв. / кварти́ра (flat)

Listen to these people from Tverskaya Street and fill in the number of the block and and flat in which they live. The first one has been done for you.

*a*  **д.**   13    **кв.**   89    *b*  **д.**       **кв.**

*c*  **д.**       **кв.**       *d*  **д.**       **кв.**

# Put it all together

1 You are turning into **улица Чéхова** from **Тверскáя улица**. Where are the following places situated? Write the letters in the right places on the map.

*a* **Теáтр напрáво**    *b* **Пóчта налéво**    *c* **Метрó прямо**

Тверскáя улица

улица Чéхова

2 Work out the following times and distances:

*a* трúдцать пять киломéтров
*b* пятьдесят однá минýта
*c* сóрок вóсемь минýт
*d* девянóсто две минýты
*e* шестьдесят одúн киломéтр
*f* вóсемьдесят три киломéтра

3 Unscramble the letters to find the following:

*a* a town
*b* a number
*c* a form of transport
*d* a direction

ýгПтеребр
кроóс
рóтме
ярмоп

4 Match the questions to the answers:

*1* **Где музéй?**            *a* **Нет, пять минýт автóбусом.**
*2* **Это далекó?**           *b* **Нет, в Нóвгороде.**
*3* **Где ты живёшь?**        *c* **Идúте напрáво.**
*4* **Вы живёте в Москвé?**   *d* **Я живý в Манчéстере.**

# Now you're talking!

1   Outside the hotel you see Anna, the tour guide. You need to ask her where a few places are.

◆ Say 'excuse me' and ask her where the underground is.
◇ **Метро? Иди́те нале́во.**
◆ Ask if it's far.
◇ **Нет, пять мину́т пешко́м.**
◆ Now ask her where the post office is.
◇ **По́чта? Иди́те пря́мо.**
◆ Thank her.

2   Imagine you're Mike Simpson on holiday in St Petersburg. You're looking a bit lost when a friendly Russian approaches you.

◇ **Вы ру́сский?**
◆ Say no, you're American, and ask if he's Russian.
◇ **Да, я ру́сский.**
◆ Ask him if he lives in St Petersburg.
◇ **Да. Где вы живёте?**
◆ Tell him you live in New York.
◇ **А . . . , хорошо́.**
◆ Ask him to direct you to the Hermitage Museum.
◇ **Эрмита́ж? Иди́те нале́во и пря́мо.**
◆ Ask if it's far.
◇ **Нет, де́сять мину́т пешко́м.**
◆ Thank him and say goodbye.

# Quiz

1  If you were told to go **напра́во**, would you go left or right?
2  Would you put *a* **оди́н** or *b* **одна́** in front of **по́чта** to explain that there is one post office in your town?
3  Which word would not be used for 'Excuse me'?
   *a* **Иди́те**  *b* **Прости́те**  *c* **Скажи́те**
4  What is the difference in meaning between:
   *a* **теа́тр** and *b* **теа́тры**?
5  If you travel by bus do you go:
   *a* **пешко́м**?  *b* **авто́бусом**?
6  Where would you live if you lived **в кварти́ре**?
7  Which of the following numbers is not divisible by five?
   *a* **сто**  *b* **пятьдеся́т пять**  *c* **со́рок два**

# Now check whether you can . . .

■ ask where something is

■ ask if it's far

■ understand basic directions

■ say where you live

■ ask someone where they live

■ use the numbers 21 to 199

Practise your Russian at every opportunity. As you walk down any street, say the house numbers to yourself. When you're in town, try to name the places you know in Russian. Whenever you change direction say **нале́во, пря́мо** or **напра́во** to yourself.

Remember, don't worry about words changing their endings – just memorize the basic word to make yourself understood.

# 6 шесть

# Это открыто?

- understanding what there is in town
  ... and when it's open
- making simple enquiries
- asking for help to understand

### В России . . .

to obtain **информация** (information) about a
town and its amenities, ask at the **сервис-бюро**
(service desk) in a hotel. This should be easy to locate
as it now usually has the sign in English: **INFORMATION**.
All large and even some small hotels give you details
of tourist attractions and opening times of museums,
theatres and shops. Museum opening times vary but
many shops are open seven days a week. The sign
**Выходной день** (day off) tells you on which days
things are closed.

# Understanding what there is in town . . .

1 Listen to these key phrases.

| | |
|---|---|
| **Вот . . .** | Here's . . . |
| **. . . план го́рода** | . . . a map of the town |
| **Здесь есть . . .** | Here, there is / are . . . |
| **. . . банк** | . . . a bank |
| **Здесь нет . . .** | Here, there isn't / aren't . . . |
| **в це́нтре** | in the centre |

2 Can you match the Russian words below with the English equivalents?
Many are very similar and you will probably be able to guess the
meaning, others you may have to look up in the glossary. Some
resemble words from other languages.

| | |
|---|---|
| банк | магази́н |
| библиоте́ка | универма́г |
| апте́ка | суперма́ркет |
| кино́ | бассе́йн |
| буфе́т | парк |
| галере́я | ры́нок |

park
snackbar
bank
swimming pool
shop
market

gallery
department store
cinema
supermarket
library
chemist's

3 Anna tells a group of tourists about some of the amenities **в го́роде**
(in town). She mentions a few of the places from the list above.
Tick them as you hear them. Where will you find a bank?

## По-ру́сски . . .

after **нет** (there isn't/aren't) nouns change their endings:

**нет ба́нка** (m.)   **нет апте́ки** (f.)   **нет вина́** (n.)

Add **-а** or **-я** for masculine and neuter singular, **-ы** or **-и** for feminine.
Many neuter nouns don't change, e.g. **нет кафе́**.

# . . . and when it's open

**4**   Listen to these key phrases.

| | |
|---|---|
| **Э́то откры́то?** | Is it open? |
| **Э́то откры́то** | It's open |
| **Э́то закры́то** | It's closed |
| **сего́дня**<br>se<u>v</u>odnya | today |

| | |
|---|---|
| **понеде́льник** (Monday)<br>пн | **четве́рг** (Thursday)<br>чт |
| **вто́рник** (Tuesday)<br>вт | **пя́тница** (Friday)<br>пт |
| **среда́** (Wednesday)<br>ср | **суббо́та** (Saturday)<br>сб |
| | **воскресе́нье** (Sunday)<br>вс |

**По-ру́сски . . .**

days of the week are often seen in their abbreviated form.

To say 'on' a particular day of the week use **в**: **в четве́рг**.

Feminine names of days change their ending from **-a** to **-y**: **в сре́ду**

**5**   Tanya is teaching her students the days of the week. She points to places on a map. Listen and decide whether the place is open or closed, and fill in the day in English.

| | откры́то | закры́то | day |
|---|---|---|---|
| *a* | | | ............................. |
| *b* | | | ............................. |
| *c* | | | ............................. |

# Making simple enquiries . . .

**1**  Listen to these key phrases.

| | |
|---|---|
| **Есть . . . ?** | Is/are there . . . ? |
| **Здесь есть . . . ?** | Is/are there . . . here? |
| **Прости́те** | Excuse me/Sorry |
| **Я не зна́ю** | I don't know |

**2**  Listen as Tanya asks in the café if there's a phone and a toilet, and decide whether the following are true or false.

| | | да | нет |
|---|---|---|---|
| a | **Здесь есть туале́т** | ▓ | ▓ |
| b | **Туале́т напра́во** | ▓ | ▓ |
| c | **Нет телефо́на** | ▓ | ▓ |

**3**  Later in the street she asks a passer-by the way. Which of the following words does he use to say he doesn't know?

    a **Я не ру́сский**    b **Я не жена́т**    c **Я не зна́ю**

**4**  She tries again. Listen out for **пото́м** (then). Make a note of the instructions in English. Where does she want to go, and is it open?

## По-ру́сски . . .

to say 'it is' simply use **он** (m.) **она́** (f.) **оно́** (n.)
to say 'they are' use **они́**

You can turn these into questions without changing the word order, just by adding a question mark and making it *sound* like a question.
**Она́ откры́та?** Is it (f.) open?
**Они́ в це́нтре?** Are they in the centre?

# . . . and asking for help to understand

**5** Listen to these key phrases.

| | |
|---|---|
| **Повторите, пожалуйста** | Please repeat that |
| **Говорите, пожалуйста, медленно** | Speak slowly, please |
| **Я не понимаю** | I don't understand |

**6** David, one of Olga's students, is in the town centre, asking the way. Listen, and fill in the letters of the missing words in the gaps. **на улице Чехова** means 'in Chekhov Street'.

| | |
|---|---|
| David | ................, пожалуйста, где здесь библиотека? |
| Passer-by | **В центре, на улице Чехова.** |
| David | **Простите, я не понимаю.** |
| | **Повторите, пожалуйста.** |
| Passer-by | **Библиотека в ................, на улице Чехова.** |
| David | **Спасибо. Она открыта во вторник?** |
| Passer-by | **Да, она ................** |
| David | **А здесь есть банк?** |
| Passer-by | **Есть.** |
| David | **Он открыт?** |
| Passer-by | **Нет, сегодня ................** |
| David | **Говорите, пожалуйста,** |
| | **................** |
| Passer-by | **................ банк закрыт.** |
| David | **Спасибо.** |
| Passer-by | **................** |

*a* открыта
*b* Сегодня
*c* Пожалуйста
*d* Скажите
*e* медленно
*f* центре
*g* закрыт

---

## По-русски . . .

**открыт** and **закрыт** must agree with the word they describe, i.e. take a masculine, feminine or neuter form:

| | | |
|---|---|---|
| **буфет открыт** | **аптека открыта** | **кафе открыто** |
| **буфет закрыт** | **аптека закрыта** | **кафе закрыто** |

# Put it all together

1 Read the following notices and answer the questions.

Третьяко́вская галере́я

метро́: Третьяко́вская
откры́та: вт–вс 10.00–18.30
выходно́й день: понеде́льник

Апте́ка Фармако́н

метро́: Тверска́я
откры́та: пн–сб 08.30–20.00

Музе́й Пу́шкина

метро́: Кропо́ткинская
откры́т: вт–пт 10.00–16.00
сб-вс 12.00–18.00

a On which day is the Tretyakov Gallery closed?
b When is the Pushkin Museum open from 10.00 to 16.00?
c When is it open on Sundays?
d On which day is the chemist's closed?

2 Say which of the amenities mentioned in this unit there are in your home town.

e.g. **Есть парк, по́чта, .......**

3 Can you say in Russian on which days the following are open and closed in your town?

a swimming pool    b library    c post office

# Now you're talking!

I **В го́роде** (in town), you stop a man in the street to ask for some information.

◆ Say 'excuse me' and ask if there's a department store here.
◇ **Да, есть, на у́лице Пу́шкина.**
◆ Say you don't understand and ask him to repeat what he said.
◇ **Да, есть, на у́лице Пу́шкина.**
◆ Ask him if the department store is open.
◇ **Да, он откры́т.**
◆ Thank him and ask if there's a chemist's here.
◇ **Апте́ка? Иди́те напра́во, пото́м пря́мо.**
◆ Ask him to speak slowly.
◇ **Апте́ка – напра́во, пото́м пря́мо.**
◆ Repeat the instructions and then ask if it's open.
◇ **Да, она́ откры́та.**
◆ Thank the man.
◇ **Пожа́луйста.**

2 Now imagine you're showing a Russian business colleague a map of your town. You'll need to be able to:

◆ say 'here's a map of the town'
◆ tell him the shops are in the centre
◆ say there is a market here on Thursday
◆ tell him that the post office is closed on Sunday
◆ say that there isn't a bank here.

# Quiz

1  If you were told **Банк в це́нтре,** where would you find a bank?
2  If the **библиоте́ка** is **закры́та,** would the library be open or closed?
3  What would you have if someone gave you a **план го́рода**?
4  Which word should you use with **апте́ка** to say that it's closed?
    *a* **закры́т**   *b* **закры́та**   *c* **закры́то**
5  Put the following days of the week in order:
    *a* **четве́рг**   *b* **пя́тница**   *c* **среда́**
6  According to this sign, on which day is the shop closed?
    **Выходно́й день: воскресе́нье**.
7  What is the Russian for 'Repeat'?
    *a* **Повтори́те** or *b* **Говори́те**

# Now check whether you can . . .

■  tell someone what there is in a town

■  ask if something is available

■  ask if a place is open or closed

■  say you're sorry, you don't know

■  ask someone to repeat something and to speak slowly

■  recognize the names of the days of the week

Learning a new language often involves guessing the meaning of words. It doesn't always work, but it's worth a try. You may be pleasantly surprised at how many Russian words sound similar to English and other languages.

**Супермáркет** is an example of a word recently adopted into the Russian language. **Макдо́нальдс** is now a popular eating place for many Russians. Can you guess what it is?

# Ско́лько сто́ит?

- using the numbers above 200
- understanding prices
- asking for items in a shop or market

## В Росси́и . . .

if you go to the **универса́м** (self-service shop) you may not need to speak a lot of Russian. However, in more traditional stores shopping can be quite a long process. You choose your goods at the counter, where you'll be told **Плати́те в ка́ссу** (Pay at the cash desk). You tell the cashier what you intend to buy and say the price. You'll then be given a **чек** (receipt) which you finally take back to the counter to receive your purchases.

# Using the numbers above 200 . . .

1  Listen to the following numbers.

| | | | |
|---|---|---|---|
| 200 | двести | 900 | девятьсот |
| 300 | триста | 1000 | тысяча |
| 400 | четыреста | 2000 | две тысячи |
| 500 | пятьсот | 3000 | три тысячи |
| 600 | шестьсот | 4000 | четыре тысячи |
| 700 | семьсот | 5000 | пять тысяч |
| 800 | восемьсот | 6000 | шесть тысяч, etc. |

**В России . . .**

the currency is the **рубль** or **р.** (rouble). There are 100 kopecks in a rouble. A new **рубль** and **копейка** or **к.** (kopeck) have recently been introduced, lopping three zeros off the old **рубль** prices, but you may still hear people talking in old money.

2  Match the Russian price with the correct figures.

a  **пять рублей двадцать две копейки**
b  **сорок один рубль пятнадцать копеек**
c  **тысяча триста шестьдесят три рубля**

| |
|---|
| 41р. 15к. |
| 1 363р. |
| 5р. 22к. |

3  Listen to the cassette and write the prices you hear.

a ........ **р.** ........ **к.**   b ........ **р.** ........ **к.**   c ........ **р.** ........ **к.**

**По-русски . . .**

after 1 and compounds of 1 use **рубль** and **копейка**:
21р. = двадцать один рубль; 41к. = сорок одна копейка

after 2, 3, 4 and their compounds use **рубля** and **копейки**:
32р. = тридцать два рубля; 43к. = сорок три копейки

after all other numbers use **рублей** and **копеек**.

# . . . and understanding prices

**4** Listen to these key phrases.

| | |
|---|---|
| **Ско́лько сто́ит?** | How much is it? |
| **Ско́лько сто́ят?** | How much are they? |
| **У вас есть . . . ?** | Have you got . . . ? |
| **Да́йте (мне), пожа́луйста, . . .** | Could you give me . . . ? |

**5** Anna is going shopping. Read her shopping list and find out what she needs, using the glossary.

> откры́тка
> почто́вая ма́рка
> аспири́н
> фотоаппара́т
> шампа́нское
> сувени́ры

**6** First, she goes into the **апте́ка**. Listen, note what she buys, and give the price.

**7** Next, to **ГУМ** (GUM), a huge department store in Moscow, to buy something for her father's birthday. Listen and find out how much the two items cost, then circle the correct answer.

| шампа́нское | фотоаппара́т |
|---|---|
| 10р. 75к. | 500р. |
| 40р. 50к. | 1000р. |
| 255р. 50к. | 2225р. |

**8** Finally, listen to Anna in the **по́чта** and answer these questions:

- how much is a postcard?
- how many does she buy?
- how much is a stamp for America (**в Аме́рику**)?

# Asking for items in a shop . . .

1  Listen to these key phrases.

| | |
|---|---|
| **Мóжно?** | May I? |
| **Мóжно посмотрéть?** | May I have a look? |
| **Мóжно** | Yes, you may/It's possible/OK |
| **Что ещё?** | Anything else? |
| **Э́то всё** | That's all |

2  Mark is looking for something typically Russian to take home to Australia. Listen to the conversation and decide which of the following Russian souvenirs he buys.

| шáпка | икрá | матрёшка | лóжки | вóдка |
|---|---|---|---|---|

3  Listen to Mark at the cash desk (**кácса**). How much does he pay for the souvenir? What does the cashier give him as well as his change (**сдáча**)?

4  How would you ask if the shop has the following, and if you can look at it/them? Listen and follow the example.

- painted wooden spoons
  **У вас есть лóжки? Мóжно посмотрéть?**
- vodka
- caviar
- a set of Russian dolls
- a Russian hat

# . . . or market

**5** Anna goes to the market. Read her shopping list and label the food shown above with the correct letter. Use the glossary if necessary.

- *a* хлеб (батóн)
- *b* я́блоки (килогрáмм)
- *c* помидóры (полкилó)
- *d* сыр (двéсти пятьдеся́т грамм)
- *e* молокó (пакéт)

**6** Listen as Anna speaks to various traders **на ры́нке** (at the market), and number the items on her list as you hear them. What does she forget to buy?

---

**По-ру́сски . . .**

nouns change their endings when they follow numbers and quantities. It is possible to avoid these changes by saying the item first, e.g.:

**Помидóры – килогрáмм, пожáлуйста**
**Я́блоки – три, пожáлуйста**

# Put it all together

**1**  Write the following numbers in figures.

    *a*  тысяча девятьсот семнадцать
    *b*  семь тысяч четыреста девяносто шесть
    *c*  двадцать две тысячи пятьсот восемьдесят три
    *d*  пятьсот тысяч сто пятьдесят пять

**2**  Match the English with the Russian phrases.

| | | |
|---|---|---|
| *a* | Можно посмотреть? | How much is it? |
| *b* | Дайте, пожалуйста, . . . | That's all. |
| *c* | Это всё. | How much are they? |
| *d* | Сколько стоит? | Have you got . . . ? |
| *e* | У вас есть . . . ? | Could you give me . . . ? |
| *f* | Что ещё? | May I have a look? |
| *g* | Сколько стоят? | Anything else? |

**3**  Unscramble the conversation by numbering these phrases 1 to 5.

Семь рублей – килограмм.
Дайте, пожалуйста, полкило.
Сколько стоят?
Да, есть.
У вас есть помидоры?

**4**  Write the following shopping list in English.

> сыр – сто пятьдесят грамм
> батон – два
> помидоры – четыре
> минеральная вода – литр
> яблоки – полкило

# Now you're talking!

1   Imagine you're in **ГУМ**, looking for a Russian souvenir to take home.

   ◆ Greet the assistant and ask if they have any souvenirs.
   ◇ **Да. Что вы хотите?**
   ◆ Say you don't know.
   ◇ **Вот, пожа́луйста, ло́жки и́ли матрёшка.**
   ◆ Ask if you can have a look (at them).
   ◇ **Мо́жно. Вот, пожа́луйста.**
   ◆ Ask the price of the spoons.
   ◇ **Два́дцать пять рубле́й.**
   ◆ Find out the cost of the set of Russian dolls.
   ◇ **Пятьдеся́т рубле́й.**
   ◆ You decide on the spoons. Ask for them.
   ◇ **Хорошо́. Э́то всё?**
   ◆ Say yes, that's all thank you.
   ◇ **Плати́те в ка́ссу два́дцать пять рубле́й.**

2   ◆ Go to the cash desk, say 'spoons' and give the price.
   ◇ **Пожа́луйста, чек.**
   ◆ Thank the cashier.
   ◇ **Пожа́луйста.**

3   ◆ Back at the counter, say 'here's the receipt'.
   ◇ **Пожа́луйста, ло́жки.**
   ◆ Thank the assistant.
   ◇ **Пожа́луйста.**

# Quiz

1 Would you use *a* **Ско́лько сто́ит?** or *b* **Ско́лько сто́ят?** to ask the price of: **Я́блоки-четы́ре?**

2 Would you put *a* **рубль** *b* **рубля́** or *c* **рубле́й** after the number **сто четы́ре?**

3 How many **копе́йки** are there in a **рубль?**

4 What sort of shop is **ГУМ?**

5 If you are told **Плати́те в ка́ссу**, where should you go?

6 If you wanted a loaf of bread, would you ask for:
*a* **паке́т** or *b* **бато́н?**

7 To ask 'Is that all?' would the sales assistant say:
*a* **Мо́жно?** *b* **Ско́лько?** *c* **Э́то всё?**

# Now check whether you can . . .

■ use the numbers above 200

■ ask how much something costs

■ understand prices and simple quantities e.g. a kilo, a carton

■ ask for something in a shop or market

■ ask if you can look at something

When Russians speak, you may not always hear the noun ending clearly, but you'll understand the basic word. Similarly, you shouldn't worry about getting the ending wrong. You'll learn much more quickly by trying to express yourself, even if you make a few mistakes, than by saying nothing until you're word-perfect.

You can give yourself time to think by saying, for example:
**Как сказа́ть по-ру́сски?** (How do you say in Russian?)

| Listen to three people outside the Astoria Hotel being given directions. Follow their route on the map. In the spaces below write down in English the places they're looking for, and then put the corresponding letters in the correct boxes above.

a ........................... b ........................... c ...........................

2 Now listen and say whether the places they're looking for are open or closed.

a ........................... b ........................... c ...........................

**3** Listen and check whether the prices you hear are the same as the ones on the list. Tick the ones that are correct and change the ones that are wrong.

| | |
|---|---|
| во́дка – ли́тр | **40р** |
| молоко́ – паке́т | **4р 40к** |
| хлеб – бато́н | **3р 25к** |
| сыр – 300г | **2р 20к** |
| помидо́ры – полкило́ | **7р 50к** |

**4** Look at the envelope below, which has been addressed in the handwritten script. See if you can recognize any words and select the right answers below, before looking back at the printed envelope on page 47.

Now select the right answer:

| | | | |
|---|---|---|---|
| *a* | The town is: | Moscow | Minsk |
| *b* | The apartment number is: | 15 | 52 |
| *c* | The addressee is: | Petrov | Ivanov |

**5** Unscramble the anagrams to find:

a a day of the week
b something you're given at the **kácca**
c a place to live
d something worn on the head

асбубто
кче
ркатрайв
пкашá

**6** Which one would you use . . .

a Повтори́те, пожа́луйста.

b Я не понима́ю.

c Как сказа́ть по-ру́сски?

d Э́то далеко́?

e Я не зна́ю.

1 . . . to say you don't understand?
2 . . . if you don't know something?
3 . . . to find out how to say something in Russian?
4 . . . when you'd like to hear something again?
5 . . . to ask if something's far away?

**7** Match each sentence to the place in which you're most likely to hear it.

a **Ско́лько сто́ит ма́рка в Аме́рику?**
b **У вас есть аспири́н?**
c **Пи́во, пожа́луйста**
d **Мо́жно посмотре́ть сувени́ры?**
e **Я́блоки – килогра́мм, пожа́луйста**

1 апте́ка
2 по́чта
3 ры́нок
4 бар
5 ГУМ

**8** David has gone to spend a few days in St Petersburg. Read the postcard he sends to Mark, using the words below to help you. Then decide whether the statements which follow are true or false.

Дорого́й Марк,

Как дела́?
Сего́дня воскресе́нье. И вот я в
Санкт-Петербу́рге. Я живу́ в
гости́нице 'Спорт', на у́лице
Толсто́го. В гости́нице есть
бассе́йн и са́уна. Недалеко́ –
музе́й, галере́я и кино́, пять мину́т
авто́бусом, и та́кже краси́вый парк.
В це́нтре есть магази́ны,
универма́г, суперма́ркет и ры́нок.
Приве́т.　　　Дави́д

АВИА
PAR AVION
РОССИЯ 45

г. *Москва*

ул.

г.

ш.

**Дорого́й** dear (m.)
**на у́лице Толсто́го**
inTolstoy Street (Talstova)
**са́уна** sauna
**краси́вый** beautiful
**Приве́т** Regards

| | да | нет |
|---|---|---|
| *a* Дави́д в Но́вгороде. | ▮ | ▮ |
| *b* Он в гости́нице. | ▮ | ▮ |
| *c* Гости́ница на у́лице Че́хова. | ▮ | ▮ |
| *d* В гости́нице есть са́уна. | ▮ | ▮ |
| *e* Недалеко́ есть музе́й. | ▮ | ▮ |
| *f* Недалеко́ есть та́кже библиоте́ка. | ▮ | ▮ |
| *g* В це́нтре ры́нок. | ▮ | ▮ |

You'll find that sometimes Russian uses far fewer words than English, e.g. **Недалеко́ есть музе́й**, where only three words are needed to say 'Not far away there is a museum'.

Have you also noticed that some Russian words have several meanings?

**Пожа́луйста** (Please/Don't mention it/Here you are/After you)
**Мо́жно?** (Is it possible?/May I?/Can we?)
**Мо́жно** (Yes, you may/It's possible/By all means/OK)

# У вас есть свобо́дный но́мер?

- ● checking in at reception
- ● asking if there's a room free
- ● asking which floor something is on
- ● making requests

### В Росси́и . . .

it is getting easier to travel independently, although most tourists use organized package tours. **Интури́ст** (Intourist) still runs many hotels, but a large number of new, private enterprises are opening up. Some even offer accommodation in private homes, an ideal way to **говори́ть по-ру́сски** (talk Russian). If you book a **но́мер люкс** (luxury room) your room will be more like an apartment with a sofa, TV, fridge and a separate bedroom.

# Checking in at reception

1   Listen to these key phrases.

| | |
|---|---|
| **Я заказáл . . .** | I've booked (man speaking) . . . |
| **Я заказáла . . .** | I've booked (woman speaking) . . . |

**. . . нóмер люкс**

**. . . одномéстный нóмер**

**. . . двухмéстный нóмер**

**с вáнной**

**с дýшем**

| | |
|---|---|
| **Вáша фамúлия, пожáлуйста** | Your surname, please |
| **Ваш пáспорт, пожáлуйста** | Your passport, please |
| **Вот мой пáспорт** | Here's my passport |

2   Anna is in reception, helping some guests to check in. Listen and fill in their room details in English below.

| | type of room | bath/shower |
|---|---|---|
| Brown | ................................ | ................................ |
| Smith | ................................ | ................................ |
| Anderson | ................................ | ................................ |

## По-рýсски . . .

after **с** (with), singular nouns usually change as follows:
add **-ом** or **-ем** to masculine and neuter nouns
add **-ой** or **-ей** to feminine nouns
**с сáхаром** (m.)   **с вáнной** (f.)   **с винóм** (n.)

# Asking if there's a room free

1 Listen to these key phrases.

| | |
|---|---|
| **У вас есть свобо́дный но́мер?** | Have you got a room free? |
| **Како́й но́мер . . .** | What sort of room . . . |
| **. . . вы хоти́те?** | . . . do you want? |
| **На ско́лько челове́к?** | For how many people? |
| **На ско́лько дней?** | For how many days? |
| **На оди́н день** | For one day |
| **На два / три / четы́ре дня** | For two / three / four days |
| **На пять / семь дней** | For five / seven days |

2 Listen to these people, who have arrived at the hotel without a reservation. Look at their **анке́та** (registration form) and tick the correct information. **Коли́чество** means 'number'.

# Asking which floor something is on

1   Listen to these key phrases.

| | |
|---|---|
| **На како́м этаже́?** | On which floor? |
| **на пе́рвом этаже́** | on the ground (literally 1st) floor |
| **на второ́м этаже́** | on the first (literally 2nd) floor |

## В Росси́и . . .

they use the same system as the Americans to refer to different floors. When you are **на пе́рвом этаже́** (literally – on the 1st floor) you are at ground level.

| | |
|---|---|
| **на тре́тьем этаже́** | on the second (3rd) floor |
| **на четвёртом этаже́** | on the third (4th) floor |
| **на пя́том этаже́** | on the fourth (5th) floor |
| **на деся́том этаже́** | on the ninth (10th) floor |

2   Which floors are those rooms on?

*a*   **на восьмо́м этаже́** .........   *b*   **на двена́цатом этаже́** .........
*c*   **на шесто́м этаже́** .........   *d*   **на девя́том этаже́** .........

3   Listen to Anna telling some guests where their rooms are. Match each person to the correct floor.

| | | | |
|---|---|---|---|
| *1* | **Бра́ун** | *a* | **на седьмо́м этаже́** |
| *2* | **Смит** | *b* | **на оди́ннадцатом этаже́** |
| *3* | **А́ндерсон** | *c* | **на пе́рвом этаже́** |

## По-ру́сски . . .

**пе́рвый** (1st), **второ́й** (2nd), etc. change their ending, as do nouns, depending on their function in a sentence. After **на** (on) before masculine or neuter nouns the ending is usually **-ом (на пе́рвом этаже́)**, and before feminine nouns, **-ой (на пе́рвой у́лице)**.

# Making requests

**1** Listen to these key phrases.

| | |
|---|---|
| **Мо́жно . . .** | Is it possible to/May I/we . . . |
| **. . . посмотре́ть но́мер?** | . . . look at the room? |
| **. . . пообе́дать в гости́нице?** | . . . dine in the hotel? |
| **. . . заказа́ть такси́?** | . . . book a taxi? |
| **Мо́жно оплати́ть . . .** | May I/we pay . . . |
| **. . . креди́тной ка́ртой?** | . . . by credit card? |
| **. . . до́лларами / фу́нтами?** | . . . with dollars / pounds? |

**2** Listen to three people talking to the **Администра́тор** (Manager) in the hotel and answer the questions.

*a* How does the first guest want to pay?
*b* Where is the taxi rank (**стоя́нка такси́**)?
*c* On which floor is the room offered to the second guest?
*d* Where is the lift (**лифт**)?
*e* Can the third guest dine in the hotel?

---

### По-ру́сски . . .

**Мо́жно**, used on its own, means 'May I/we?' or 'You may'.
It can be followed by a verb in the infinitive (the dictionary form, usually ending in **-ть**), e.g. **Мо́жно пообе́дать?**
It can also be used with a noun to ask for something e.g.:
**Ключ мо́жно?** (May I/we have the key?)

**Ключ мо́жно?**

# Put it all together

**1** Unscramble the following conversation by numbering the phrases 1 to 8.

**Да, есть. На ско́лько дней?**
**Мо́жно. Вот ключ.**
**И на ско́лько челове́к?**
**На три дня.**
**У вас есть свобо́дный но́мер?**
**Мо́жно посмотре́ть но́мер?**
**На два.**
**Есть двухме́стный но́мер на седьмо́м этаже́.**

**2** Find the most suitable rooms for these hotel guests.

*1* **Я заказа́л но́мер с ду́шем.**
*2* **Я заказа́ла но́мер с телефо́ном.**
*3* **Я заказа́л одноме́стный но́мер.**
*4* **У вас есть но́мер люкс?**
*5* **Мо́жно посмотре́ть но́мер с ва́нной?**

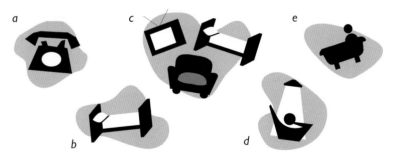

*a*  *c*  *e*

*b*  *d*

**3** Match the answers with the questions.

| | | | |
|---|---|---|---|
| *1* | **На ско́лько дней?** | *a* | **Но́мер с ва́нной.** |
| *2* | **Рестора́н на како́м этаже́?** | *b* | **На пять дней.** |
| *3* | **Како́й но́мер вы хоти́те?** | *c* | **Нет, до́лларами.** |
| *4* | **Мо́жно посмотре́ть но́мер?** | *d* | **Да, мо́жно. Вот ключ.** |
| *5* | **Мо́жно оплати́ть фу́нтами?** | *e* | **На второ́м этаже́.** |

# ❝ Now you're talking!

I  Take the part of **Мария Ивановна Петрова,** arriving at the **Гостиница 'Спутник'**.

◆ Greet the manager and ask if they have a room free.
◇ **Одноместный или двухместный номер?**
◆ Say 'a single room with a shower'.
◇ **На сколько дней?**
◆ Say 'for two days'.
◇ **Хорошо. Есть свободный номер на пятом этаже.**
◆ Ask if you can see the room.
◇ **Можно. Вот ключ.**


2  You have decided to take the room, so you return to reception.

◇ **Ваша фамилия, пожалуйста.**
◆ Give your surname.
◇ **Ваш паспорт, пожалуйста.**
◆ Say 'here's my passport'.
◇ **Спасибо.**
◆ Ask if you can dine in the hotel.
◇ **Да, ресторан открыт.**
◆ Find out on what floor the restaurant is.
◇ **На третьем этаже.**
◆ Ask if you can pay by credit card.
◇ **Да, можно.**
◆ Thank him.
◇ **Пожалуйста.**

# Quiz

1 Would a man say *a* **Я заказáл** or *b* **Я заказáла**?
2 If someone asked you for your **пáспорт**, what would you give them?
3 If your room was **на пéрвом этажé** of a Russian hotel, would you be on the ground floor or first floor?
4 Who is the **Администрáтор** in a hotel?
5 If you were asked to complete an **анкéта**, what would you be given to fill in?
6 Where would you be if you were in a **лифт**?
7 If you told someone your **фамúлия**, what would you be telling them?

# Now check whether you can . . .

- ◼ say you've booked a room

- ◼ ask if there's a room free

- ◼ specify the type of room you want

- ◼ say how long you want the room for

- ◼ ask which floor something is on

- ◼ ask to see the room

- ◼ ask about methods of payment

Looking up Russian words in a dictionary can at times seem confusing. For example, if you look up the word **нóмер** you'll find that it has several meanings:
> number (of a telephone);
> room (at a hotel);
> size (of clothes);
> item (at a concert).

You can usually work out the correct meaning from the context.

# Когда́ отхо́дит?

- asking about public transport
- finding out train times
- buying train tickets
- finding your way around the Metro

### В Росси́и . . .

there is a wide choice of public transport in towns. You can take a **трамва́й** (tram), **тролле́йбус** (trolleybus) or **авто́бус** (bus). When you buy a **тало́н** (ticket), you can travel any distance for the same price.

In Moscow and St Petersburg, as well as in some of the new republics, the **метро́** (underground) is an excellent way to travel. Again, there is only one price, but instead of a ticket, you have to buy a **жето́н** (token).

You may like to use the **по́езд** (train) to travel longer distances, and even go on the Trans-Siberian Express, the ultimate way to see Russia!

# Asking about public transport

| Listen to these key phrases.

| **Есть автобус до . . . ?** | Is there a bus to . . . ? |
|---|---|
| **Есть автобус до метро?** | Is there a bus to the Metro? |
| **Какой автобус . . .** | Which bus . . . |
| **трамвай . . .** | tram . . . |
| **троллейбус . . .** | trolleybus . . . |
| **. . . идёт до . . . ?** | . . . goes to . . . ? |

2 Listen to three people outside their hotel asking how to get to various places. Write down in English how they intend to travel, the number of the bus, tram or trolleybus, and where they want to go. Listen for the word **остановка** (bus, tram or trolleybus stop).

| Form of transport | Number | Destination |
|---|---|---|
| *a* .............................. | ............ | .............................. |
| *b* .............................. | ............ | .............................. |
| *c* .............................. | ............ | .............................. |

## По-русски . . .

**до** means 'to' (up to, as far as), and nouns that follow **до** usually change their endings as follows:
masculine and neuter singular nouns to **-а** or **-я**
**до ресторана**   to the restaurant
feminine singular nouns to **-ы** or **-и**.
**до почты**      to the post office

Words originating from other languages, e.g. **метро**, do not change.

3 Listen to the cassette. How would you ask:

- if there's a bus to the airport (**аэропорт**)?
- which trolleybus goes to the railway station (**вокзал**)?
- which tram goes to Pushkin Street (**улица Пушкина**)?

# Finding out train times

**1** Listen to these key phrases.

| | |
|---|---|
| **Когда́ отхо́дит?** | When does it leave? |
| **В кото́ром часу́ . . .** | At what time . . . |
| **. . . сле́дующий по́езд . . .** | . . . is the next train . . . |
| **. . . до Москвы́?** | . . . to Moscow? |
| **Когда́ я бу́ду в Москве́?** | When will I be in Moscow? |

**По-ру́сски . . .**

the twenty-four hour clock is widely used. To say at what time
something happens, begin with **в** (at) and use the same endings for
**час** (hour) as for **киломе́тр** on page 45.

**в час** `01:00`   **в три часа́** `03:00`   **в два́дцать часо́в** `20:00`

**в трина́дцать часо́в со́рок мину́т** `13:40`

**2** Write the following times in numbers.

    *a*   **два́дцать оди́н час пятна́дцать мину́т**
    *b*   **семна́дцать часо́в два́дцать одна́ мину́та**
    *c*   **два́дцать два часа́ со́рок три мину́ты**
    *d*   **шесть часо́в три́дцать пять мину́т**

**3** Listen to people at the **спра́вочное бюро́** (enquiry office) asking
about train times, and fill in the missing departure and arrival times.

| | **Отправле́ние** (Departure) | **Прибы́тие** (Arrival) |
|---|---|---|
| **Оде́сса** | .............................. | .............................. |
| **Я́лта** | .............................. | .............................. |
| **Ки́ев** | .............................. | .............................. |

# Buying train tickets

**1** Listen to these key phrases.

| | |
|---|---|
| **Один билéт / два билéта до . . .** | One / two tickets to . . . |
| **Билéт в одúн конéц . . .** | A single ticket . . . |
| **. . . úли тудá и обрáтно?** | . . . or return? |
| **С какóй платфóрмы . . .** | From which platform . . . |
| **. . . отхóдит пóезд?** | . . . does the train leave? |

**2** Listen to four people buying train tickets, and decide whether they want a single or return.

| | в одúн конéц | тудá и обрáтно |
|---|---|---|
| **Москвá** | ▬ | ▬ |
| **Нóвгород** | ▬ | ▬ |
| **Одéсса** | ▬ | ▬ |
| **Ялта** | ▬ | ▬ |

**3** Listen to these passengers at the **спрáвочное бюрó** asking which platform they need. Make a note in English of their destinations and the platform numbers.

| | destination | platform |
|---|---|---|
| *a* | ................................ | ..................... |
| *b* | ................................ | ..................... |
| *c* | ................................ | ..................... |
| *d* | ................................ | ..................... |

# Finding your way around the Metro

1 Listen to these key phrases.

| | |
|---|---|
| **Следующая станция . . .** | The next Metro station is . . . |
| **Вот схема метро** | Here's a plan of the Metro |
| **Надо . . .** | Do you/I have to . . . |
| **. . . купить жетон?** | . . . buy a token? |
| **. . . делать пересадку?** | . . . make a change? |
| **Когда надо выходить?** | When do I have to get off? |

2 Mark is travelling on the Moscow underground for the first time. He isn't sure whether he has to buy a ticket, so he asks a Russian woman, who is very helpful and accompanies him on the train. Listen and decide whether the following statements are true or not.

| | | да | нет |
|---|---|---|---|
| *a* | **Надо купить билет** | ▩ | ▩ |
| *b* | **Надо делать пересадку** | ▩ | ▩ |
| *c* | **Следующая станция Киевская** | ▩ | ▩ |

3 On the train, Mark hears some announcements, which tell him the station he's at, to be careful as the doors are closing, and the name of the next station:

**'Станция Бауманская . . . Осторожно, двери закрываются. Следующая станция Сретенский Бульвар.'**

Listen, and as you hear them, number 1 to 4 each station he arrives at.

| | |
|---|---|
| **Площадь Революции** | . . . . . . . . . . . . . . . |
| **Смоленская** | . . . . . . . . . . . . . . . |
| **Киевская** | . . . . . . . . . . . . . . . |
| **Арбатская** | . . . . . . . . . . . . . . . |

# Put it all together

**|**   Select the answer for each question.

    *|*   **На́до купи́ть биле́т?**
    *2*   **С како́й платфо́рмы отхо́дит по́езд?**
    *3*   **Како́й тролле́йбус идёт до Эрмита́жа?**
    *4*   **Како́й биле́т вы хоти́те?**
    *5*   **Есть авто́бус до метро́?**

       *a*   **Тролле́йбус но́мер три́дцать.**
       *b*   **Есть. Вот напра́во – остано́вка.**
       *c*   **Нет, в метро́ на́до купи́ть жето́н.**
       *d*   **В оди́н коне́ц, пожа́луйста.**
       *e*   **С платфо́рмы но́мер шесть.**

**2**   Work out how you would say the following in Russian, using the twenty-four hour clock.

    *a*   at 01.00        *b*   at 13.00
    *c*   at 04.00        *d*   at 16.00
    *e*   at 07.10        *f*   at 19.10

**3**   Choose the correct ending for each sentence.

    *|*   **Осторо́жно, две́ри**     *a*   **Арба́тская.**
    *2*   **На́до де́лать**     *b*   **отхо́дит в семь часо́в.**
    *3*   **По́езд до Ки́ева**     *c*   **девяно́сто рубле́й.**
    *4*   **Сле́дующая ста́нция**     *d*   **закрыва́ются.**
    *5*   **Биле́т сто́ит**     *e*   **переса́дку.**

**4**   Unscramble the letters to find four forms of transport.

    *a*   **во́сбаут**
    *b*   **до́зпе**
    *c*   **лртбли́се́уо**
    *d*   **ймтава́р**

# Now you're talking!

1   Imagine you're outside your hotel, talking to your guide. She has just
    recommended a visit to the **Арба́т,** a popular shopping precinct
    in the centre of Moscow.

  ◆ Ask if it's far.
  ◇ **Нет, де́сять мину́т тролле́йбусом.**
  ◆ Ask which trolleybus.
  ◇ **Тролле́йбус но́мер два́дцать шесть.**
  ◆ Find out where the trolleybus stop is.
  ◇ **Вот нале́во – остано́вка.**

2   After your visit to the **Арба́т,** you decide to travel back on the
    Metro.

  ◆ At the enquiry office, ask where Kievskaya station is.
  ◇ **Вот схе́ма метро́ и вот – Ки́евская.**
  ◆ Ask if you have to change.
  ◇ **Нет, не на́до.**

3   The next day you want to travel to St Petersburg on the overnight
    train.

  ◆ At the ticket office, ask for a single ticket to St. Petersburg.
  ◇ **Девяно́сто рубле́й.**
  ◆ Find out the time of the next train.
  ◇ **В два́дцать два часа́.**
  ◆ Ask what platform the train leaves from.
  ◇ **С платфо́рмы но́мер двена́дцать.**

# Quiz

1  Is **жетóн** the word for a bus ticket or a Metro token?
2  What type of transport would you use at the **аэропóрт**?
3  Why would you go to the **спрáвочное бюрó**?
4  What is the difference between *a* **вокзáл** and *b* **стáнция метрó**?
5  If you were at an **останóвка** which of the following would you *not* be waiting for?

   *a* **трамвáй**   *b* **пóезд**   *c* **троллéйбус**
6  What sort of ticket is a **билéт тудá и обрáтно**?
7  If you are told **Нáдо дéлать пересáдку** what would you need to do?

# Now check whether you can . . .

■  ask which tram, trolleybus, bus goes to a particular place

■  ask what time trains (or other means of transport) depart

■  find out when you'll be in a particular place

■  find out what platform a train leaves from

■  ask for a single or return ticket

■  find out if you have to change

■  understand announcements on the Metro

When learning a language it can be very easy to underestimate how much you know. Go back occasionally to one of the early units to prove to yourself how much you've learnt. Remember how difficult the word **Здрáвствуйте** seemed when you first met it. A good tip to help you 'Talk Russian' is to paraphrase, i.e. simplify what you want to say, and avoid saying anything too complicated.

# Прия́тного аппети́та!

- reading the menu
- asking what's available
- ordering a meal
- saying what you like and don't like

## В Росси́и . . .

there is quite a wide choice of eating places. If you dine in a **рестора́н** it will almost certainly have an **орке́стр** and a dance floor. Most Russians eat out rarely, but when they do, it's not just for a meal, but rather for a real celebration where the vodka flows.

A number of restaurants offer **традицио́нная ру́сская ку́хня** (traditional Russian cooking), while others specialize in **национа́льные блю́да** (national dishes) from one of the regional restaurants such as the **Узбекиста́н** (Uzbekistan).

In a restaurant, you will often be wished **Прия́тного аппети́та!** (Enjoy your meal!).

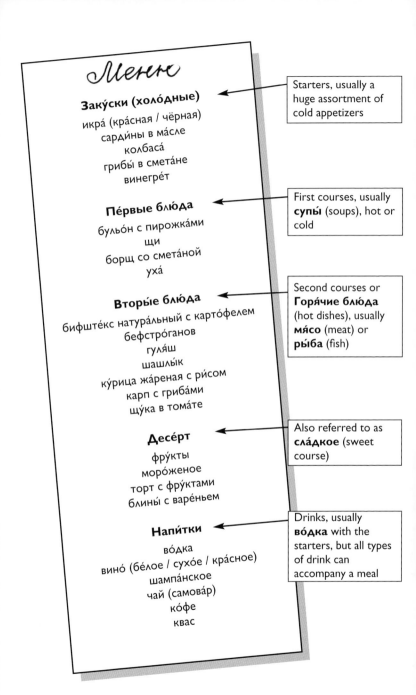

## Меню́

### Заку́ски (холо́дные)

икра́ (кра́сная / чёрная)
сарди́ны в ма́сле
колбаса́
грибы́ в смета́не
винегре́т

Starters, usually a huge assortment of cold appetizers

### Пе́рвые блю́да

бульо́н с пирожка́ми
щи
борщ со смета́ной
уха́

First courses, usually **супы́** (soups), hot or cold

### Вторы́е блю́да

бифште́кс натура́льный с карто́фелем
бефстро́ганов
гуля́ш
шашлы́к
ку́рица жа́реная с ри́сом
карп с гриба́ми
щу́ка в тома́те

Second courses or **Горя́чие блю́да** (hot dishes), usually **мя́со** (meat) or **ры́ба** (fish)

### Десе́рт

фру́кты
моро́женое
торт с фру́ктами
блины́ с варе́ньем

Also referred to as **сла́дкое** (sweet course)

### Напи́тки

во́дка
вино́ (бе́лое / сухо́е / кра́сное)
шампа́нское
чай (самова́р)
ко́фе
квас

Drinks, usually **во́дка** with the starters, but all types of drink can accompany a meal

# Reading the menu

Read through the following notes, then read the menu. Consult the glossary for any words you can't guess.

Drinks and dishes are often described by adjectives, which have to agree with the noun they describe:

| | |
|---|---|
| **бифштéкс натурáльный** (m.) | beefsteak – grilled |
| **крáсная икрá** (f.) | red caviar (cheaper than black caviar) |
| **бéлое винó** (n.) | white wine |
| **холóдные закýски** (plural) | cold starters |

The following adjectives are worth knowing:

| | | | |
|---|---|---|---|
| **горячий** | hot | **жáреный** | fried/roasted |
| **чёрный** | black | **слáдкий** | sweet |

Usually the main course comes already garnished **с гарнúром** but sometimes the vegetables or sauce may be specified using:

**с** (with) + endings on page 72 – or
**в** (in) + endings on page 46.

| | |
|---|---|
| **чай с лимóном** (m.) | tea with lemon |
| **борщ со сметáной** (f.) | beetroot soup with sour cream |
| **блины́ с варéньем** (n.) | pancakes with jam |
| **карп с грибáми** (pl.) | carp with mushrooms |
| **щýка в томáте** (m.) | pike in tomato sauce |
| **грибы́ в сметáне** (f.) | mushrooms in sour cream |
| **сардúны в мáсле** (n.) | sardines in oil/butter |

Traditionally, for dessert, Russians often heat the **самовáр** and drink **чай** with **варéнье** (jam).

# Asking what's available

1  Listen to these key phrases.

| | |
|---|---|
| **Да́йте, пожа́луйста, меню́** | Give me a menu, please |
| **Каки́е заку́ски у вас есть?** | What starters have you got? |
| **Что у вас есть сего́дня . . .** | What have you got today . . . |
| **. . . на пе́рвое?** | . . . for the first course? |
| **. . . на второ́е?** | . . . for the main course? |
| **. . . на десе́рт?** | . . . for dessert? |

2  Anna and Ivan are in the restaurant '**Моско́вский**'. Listen out for the polite way to call the waiter, '**Молодо́й челове́к**', and write down in English what they ask him for.

3  Listen as they ask what starters are available today, and number the items as you hear them. Listen out for the word **то́лько** (only). Which of their starters is not available?

| | | | |
|---|---|---|---|
| a | **кра́сная икра́** | b | **чёрная икра́** |
| c | **сарди́ны в ма́сле** | d | **колбаса́** |
| e | **грибы́ в смета́не** | f | **винегре́т** |

4  They ask what soup there is. Listen and say what sort of soup Anna wants.

5  Listen as the waiter tells them what's on offer for the main course and say whether the following are true or false:

| | | да | нет |
|---|---|---|---|
| a | **Есть шашлы́к** | ▭ | ▭ |
| b | **Есть щу́ка с гриба́ми** | ▭ | ▭ |
| c | **Есть ку́рица с карто́фелем** | ▭ | ▭ |
| d | **Есть бефстро́ганов** | ▭ | ▭ |

# Ordering a meal

1   Listen to these key phrases.

| | |
|---|---|
| **Слушаю вас** | At your service (I'm listening) |
| **Что вы рекомендуете?** | What do you recommend? |
| **Что вы будете есть?** | What will you have to eat? |
| **Что вы будете пить?** | What will you have to drink? |
| **Счёт, пожалуйста** | The bill, please |

2   Another customer at the restaurant is ready to order his meal. Listen as he calls the waitress, '**Девушка**'. Tick what he orders from the menu on page 88.

**По-русски ...**

feminine singular nouns e.g. **курица** change their ending from **-a** to **-y** when they are the object of a verb.

| | |
|---|---|
| **Дайте мне курицу.** | Give me the chicken. |
| **Дайте мне матрёшку.** | Give me the set of dolls. |

Here **курицу** and **матрёшку** are the objects of the verb 'give'.

| | |
|---|---|
| **Что вы будете есть?** | What will you have to eat? |
| **Курицу, пожалуйста.** | Chicken, please |

Here **курицу** is the object of the verb 'I'll have/eat'.

3   Listen as the same customer orders a drink, and say in English what he asks for. Circle the Russian word he uses.

**Водка**          **Водку**

4   After his meal he asks for the bill. Listen, and choose the correct amount below:

*a*   **250 рублей**        *b*   **275 рублей**        *c*   **175 рублей**

# Saying what you like . . .

**1** Listen to these key phrases.

| | |
|---|---|
| **Мне нра́вится . . .** | I like . . . |
| **Вам нра́вится . . . ?** | Do you like . . . ? (formal) |
| **Тебе́ нра́вится . . . ?** | Do you like . . . ? (informal) |

**2** A family in the Restaurant '**Салю́т**' are having a meal. Listen as they discuss the main courses, and draw a line to match each person to the dish they like.

**па́па (Ми́ша)**      **ма́ма**      **сын (Пётр)**      **дочь (Ната́ша)**

*a* **ры́ба**   *b* **бифште́кс**   *c* **бефстро́ганов**   *d* **карп**

---

### По-ру́сски . . .

to talk about liking something which is plural, you replace **нра́вится** with **нра́вятся,** but they sound very similar.

| | |
|---|---|
| **Вам нра́вятся сарди́ны?** | Do you like sardines? |
| **Тебе́ нра́вятся грибы́?** | Do you like mushrooms? |
| **Да, мне нра́вятся** | Yes, I like them |

---

**3** How would you say you like the following? Check with the recording.

- caviar   - pancakes   - red wine   - cold starters

# . . . and don't like

**4** Listen to these key phrases.

| | |
|---|---|
| **Мне не нра́вится . . .** | I don't like . . . |
| **Мне о́чень нра́вится . . .** | I like . . . very much |
| **Мне бо́льше нра́вится . . .** | I prefer . . . |
| **Э́то о́чень вку́сно** | This is/It's very tasty |

**5** Listen as the waiter begins to take their order for starters, and write down in English what the mother orders.

**6** The father and son now choose their starters. Listen out for the word **коне́чно** (of course), and tick the dish they ask for.

| | |
|---|---|
| **па́па:** | **винегре́т / сала́т** |
| **сын:** | **кра́сная икра́ / чёрная икра́** |

**7** Listen and note down in English why the daughter doesn't want a starter. Listen out for the word **ничего́** (nothing), which is a useful little word, also used to mean 'not bad/never mind'.

**8** The **метрдоте́ль** (head waiter) comes to ask if everything is all right. **'Всё норма́льно?'** Listen and fit the letter of the missing word into the appropriate gap.

| | |
|---|---|
| Метрдоте́ль | ............... **норма́льно?** |
| Па́па | ..............., **спаси́бо.** |
| Метрдоте́ль | **Тебе́** ............... **десе́рт?** |
| Пётр | **Да, э́то о́чень** ................ |

*a* **нра́вится**
*b* **Всё**
*c* **вку́сно**
*d* **Да**

# Put it all together

1  Match the English with the Russian phrases.

| | | |
|---|---|---|
| *a* | **с варéньем** | fried |
| *b* | **в томáте** | with mushrooms |
| *c* | **жáреный** | in butter |
| *d* | **в мáсле** | tasty |
| *e* | **с гарнúром** | with jam |
| *f* | **с грибáми** | garnished with vegetables |
| *g* | **вкýсно** | in tomato sauce |

2  Put the letters for the following dishes in the correct columns.

| закýски | пéрвые блюда | вторы́е блюда | десéрт |
|---|---|---|---|
| ·········· | ·········· | ·········· | ·········· |
| ·········· | ·········· | ·········· | ·········· |
| ·········· | ·········· | ·········· | ·········· |

*a* **торт**  *b* **шашлы́к**  *c* **кýрица**        *d* **икрá**  *e* **щýка**
*f* **я́блоки** *g* **борщ**  *h* **морóженое** *i* **щи**  *j* **винегрéт**

3  How would you say you like the following?

*a* **колбасá**  *b* **помидóры**  *c* **рýсские закýски**

Now how would you say you don't like them?

4  Unscramble the following dialogue by numbering the phrases 1 to 5.

**Хорошó. Дáйте мне, пожáлуйста, торт.**
**Торт с фрýктами. Э́то óчень вкýсно.**
**Слýшаю вас.**
**Молодóй человéк!**
**Что вы рекомендýете на десéрт?**

# Now you're talking!

1 Imagine you're at the **ресторáн 'Москóвский'** for a meal.

  ◆ Call the waiter and ask for the menu.
  ◇ **Вот меню́.**
  ◆ Thank him.
  ◇ **Пожáлуйста.**


2 He returns a few minutes later to take your order.

  ◇ **Слу́шаю вас.**
  ◆ Ask for sardines in oil.
  ◇ **А на пéрвое?**
  ◆ Order beetroot soup.
  ◇ **Хорошó, а на вторóе?**
  ◆ Say you like fish and ask what he recommends.
  ◇ **Сегóдня есть карп с грибáми. Э́то óчень вку́сно.**
  ◆ Order the carp with mushrooms.
  ◇ **Что вы бу́дете пить?**
  ◆ Ask him to give you a white wine.


3 He comes back while you're eating your main meal.

  ◇ **Всё нормáльно? Вам нрáвится карп?**
  ◆ Tell him that you like it very much.
  ◇ **Что вы бу́дете на десéрт?**
  ◆ Say 'nothing' and explain that you don't like dessert.

# Quiz

1 What would you be given if you asked for the **меню**?
2 If you want to call the waiter, would you say:
  *a* **Дéвушка!** or *b* **Молодóй человéк!** ?
3 Put the following dishes in the order you normally eat them:
  *a* **вторóе** *b* **слáдкое** *c* **пéрвое** *d* **закýски**
4 If the waitress says: **Слýшаю вас,** what should you do?
5 What drink do you associate with a **самовáр**?
6 To say you like **блины́** would you use:
  *a* **мне нрáвится** or *b* **мне нрáвятся**?
7 Which is the odd one out?
  *a* **мя́со** *b* **ры́ба** *c* **квас** *d* **колбасá**

# Now check whether you can . . .

■ understand the main points of a Russian menu

■ ask what dishes are available

■ order a meal with drinks

■ say what you like and what you don't like

**Брáво!** Well done! You have reached the end of Talk Russian.

And now . . . prepare yourself for **Контрóльная рабóта 3**
(checkpoint 3) with some revision. Listen to the conversations again
– the more you listen the more confident you will become. You can
test your knowledge of the key phrases by covering up the English on
the lists. Look back at the final pages of each unit and use the quizzes
and checklists to assess how much you remember.

Take every opportunity to speak Russian; if no one else is available,
talk out loud to yourself.

# Контро́льная рабо́та 3

**1** In the **спра́вочное бюро́** at the **вокза́л** you hear people asking about train times. Listen and match the train numbers to the correct times.

a   по́езд но́мер 13      b   по́езд но́мер 6
c   по́езд но́мер 20      d   по́езд но́мер 8

| 10:10 |   | 07:30 |   | 21:15 |   | 23.50 |

**2** You need a drink, so you ask someone where the snack-bar is. Which of these questions would you ask?

a   Скажи́те, пожа́луйста, где гости́ница?
b   Скажи́те, пожа́луйста, здесь есть буфе́т?
c   Скажи́те, пожа́луйста, здесь есть магази́н?

**3** The person you ask replies: **Вот нале́во – буфе́т.**
Should you turn to your left or your right?

**4** In the **буфе́т** you look at the drinks available.

a   Tick all the cold, non-alcoholic drinks
b   How would you ask for a tea with lemon?

Напитки

вино́           ко́фе              пи́во
ви́ски          лимона́д           тома́тный сок
во́дка          минера́льная вода́ фа́нта
квас           молоко́            чай
конья́к         пе́пси-ко́ла        шампа́нское

**5** The man standing next to you looks very friendly, so you decide to try out your Russian. Check your answers with the recordings.

    *a*   Greet him and tell him you're English.

    *b*   Ask him if he's Russian and where he lives.

    *c*   Tell him you like Moscow very much.

**6** You then ask him where the **Гости́ница 'Пра́га'** is. Listen and write down in English the directions he gives you.

**7** You've found the **Гости́ница 'Пра́га'**. At reception you are waiting behind a woman who says she's booked a double room with a shower. Which of the following do you hear her say?

    *a*   **Я заказа́л одноме́стный но́мер с ду́шем**

    *b*   **Я заказа́л одноме́стный но́мер с ва́нной**

    *c*   **Я заказа́ла двухме́стный но́мер с ду́шем**

    *d*   **Я заказа́ла но́мер люкс**

**8** The receptionist tells her that her room is:
**на четвёртом этаже́**

What floor would she be on?

**9** While you're waiting at reception, you see lots of Russian signs. Look at the following and say what they mean.

**10** Now it's your turn to check in. You'll need to know how to:

- say that you've booked a single room with a bath for 3 days
- ask if you can dine in the hotel
- check which floor the restaurant is on
- make sure that you can pay by credit card

**11** Later, you dine in the hotel restaurant, very keen to try **традицио́нная ру́сская ку́хня**. Listen to the recordings. You'll need to know how to ask for the following:

- mushrooms in sour cream
- clear soup with pasties
- lamb kebabs
- pancakes with jam
- a Russian soft drink made from black bread and yeast

12   After your meal you go to the **бар** for a drink. You pick up a
     children's magazine, '**Весёлые Картинки**' (literally 'Jolly Pictures')
     and see the following quiz page. You have to match a word from the
     left column with one from the right. Try it!

| | | | |
|---|---|---|---|
| 1 | **рубль** | ● | **дом** |
| 2 | **бассéйн** | ● | **чек** |
| 3 | **бар** | ● | **музéй** |
| 4 | **мáрка** | ● | **закрыт** |
| 5 | **квартира** | ● | **водá** |
| 6 | **кáсса** | ● | **банк** |
| 7 | **Эрмитáж** | ● | **кафé** |
| 8 | **открыт** | ● | **открытка** |

13   Now try the word search before going up to your **нóмер**.

| | | |
|---|---|---|
| аптéка | кóфе | спаси́бо |
| до свидáния | открыто | у́лица |
| здрáвствуйте | пóчта | центр |
| кафé | ресторáн | что |

| а | н | ц | у | е | т | й | у | в | т | с | в | а | р | д | з | а |
|---|---|---|---|---|---|---|---|---|---|---|---|---|---|---|---|---|
| я | к | а | е | н | г | ш | щ | л | з | х | ф | ы | в | а | п | р |
| и | о | л | р | д | б | э | я | ч | и | с | м | и | т | б | ю | ж |
| н | ь | ь | ё | о | ц | р | т | н | е | ц | у | к | е | н | г | ш |
| а | а | в | ы | ф | т | д | л | о | р | п | а | п | т | е | к | а |
| д | н | с | ч | я | э | с | у | в | т | с | в | о | р | д | з | а |
| и | т | и | м | с | п | й | е | т | б | о | т | ч | ю | ё | й | ц |
| в | е | к | у | а | т | й | у | р | т | с | в | т | р | е | н | г |
| с | н | а | с | е | е | ф | о | к | л | о | р | а | л | д | э | ж |
| о | т | и | а | м | и | т | р | в | а | х | щ | г | п | т | о | я |
| д | б | а | ф | е | т | ы | щ | э | ы | ф | т | м | н | у | я | г |
| о | в | п | х | д | т | й | и | л | ю | щ | е | о | м | ш | а | е |
| в | ё | п | х | о | т | ы | у | р | н | э | д | к | и | л | х | ш |

# Audio scripts and answers

This section contains scripts of all the conversations. Answers which consist of words and phrases from the conversations are given in bold type in the scripts. Other answers are given separately.

## Unit 1 Здравствуйте!

### Pages 8 & 9 Saying hello, goodbye and how are you

2 • **Здравствуйте.**
• Здравствуйте.

3 • Здравствуйте.
• Здравствуйте.
• **Здравствуй.**
• Здравствуйте.
• **Здравствуй.**
*There are 2 young people/children.*

4 • Здравствуйте. *(1 hello)*
• Здравствуйте. *(2 hello)*
• До свидания. *(3 goodbye)*
• Здравствуйте. *(4 hello)*
• До свидания. *(5 goodbye)*

6 • Здравствуйте. Как у вас дела?
• Спасибо, хорошо. А как у вас?
• Спасибо, хорошо.
*How are you?*

7 • Как дела?
• Спасибо, хорошо.
*Fine, thank you.*

8 *1* До свидания.
*2* А как у вас?
*3* Здравствуйте.
*4* Спасибо, хорошо.
*5* Как у вас дела?
*6* Здравствуй.

### Pages 10 & 11 Introducing yourself and asking someone's name

2 • Здравствуйте. Меня зовут Ольга.
• Меня зовут Иван.
• Меня зовут Таня.
• А меня зовут Виктор.
*Olga, Ivan, Tanya, Victor.*

4 • Здравствуйте. Как вас зовут?
• Меня зовут Виктор.
• **Простите?**
• Меня зовут Виктор.
• **Очень рада.**
• Очень рад.
*She says 'Очень рада' because a woman says 'pleased to meet you' in a different way from a man.*

5 | | |
|---|---|
| Anna | Здравствуйте. |
| Tanya | *(b)* **Здравствуйте.** |
| Anna | Как *(d)* **вас** зовут? |
| Tanya | Меня зовут Таня. |
| | *(a)* **Как** вас зовут? |
| Anna | *(e)* **Меня** зовут Анна, а как тебя зовут? |
| Boris | Меня зовут Борис. |
| Anna | Очень рада. |
| Boris | *(c)* **Очень** рад. |

6 *1* Меня зовут Анна.
*2* Как вас зовут?
*3* Очень рад.
*4* Как тебя зовут?
*5* Простите?
*6* Как дела?

### Page 12 Put it all together

2 *a* but/and; *b* how; *c* mum; *d* tact; *e* atom; *f* coma; *g* attack; *h* comet.

3 *a* underground/metro; *b* theatre; *c* restaurant; *d* tractor; *e* course; *f* Moscow; *g* orchestra; *h* character.

**4** *a* Goodbye; *b* What's your name?;
*c* My name's Anna; *d* Pleased to
meet you; *e* How are you?

## Page 13 **Now you're talking!**

1 • **Здра́вствуйте.**
  • Здра́вствуйте. Как у вас дела́?
  • **Спаси́бо, хорошо́. А как у
    вас?**
  • Спаси́бо, хорошо́.

  • **Здра́вствуйте. Меня́ зову́т
    + *your name*.**
  • О́чень рад. Меня́ зову́т Ива́н.
  • **Прости́те?**
  • Меня́ зову́т Ива́н.
  • **До свида́ния.**

2 • **Здра́вствуйте.**
  • Здра́вствуйте.
  • **Здра́вствуй.**
  • Здра́вствуйте.
  • **Как тебя́ зову́т?**
  • Меня́ зову́т Са́ша.
  • **Как дела́?**
  • Спаси́бо, хорошо́.

3 • **Здра́вствуйте.**
  • **Как вас зову́т?**
  • **Как у вас дела́?**
  • **До свида́ния.**

## Page 14 **Quiz**

*1* c; *2* Moscow; *3* His mum; *4* In a
restaurant; *5* b; *6* very well; *7* a; *8* b;
*9* b; *10* a.

## Unit 2 **Я англича́нин.**

### Pages 16 & 17 **Asking someone's
nationality and stating yours**

2 • Дави́д, вы америка́нец?
  • Нет, я не америка́нец. Я
    кана́дец.
  • Анн, а вы америка́нка?

  • Да, я америка́нка.
  • Ли́са, вы америка́нка?
  • Нет, я англича́нка.
  • Марк, а вы англича́нин?
  • Нет, я не англича́нин. Я
    австрали́ец
*David is Canadian; Ann is American;
Lisa is English; Mark is Australian.*

3 *a* America; *b* Canada; *c* England;
*d* Russia; *e* Britain; *f* Australia.

4 *1*d; *2*c; *3*b; *4*a; *5*f; *6*e.
*2 and 4 are women.*

5 *a* Englishman; *b* American woman;
*c* Russian man; *d* Canadian man.

### Page 18 **Saying whether you are
married**

2 • Дави́д, вы жена́ты?
  • Да, я жена́т.
  • Анн, вы за́мужем?
  • Нет, я не за́мужем.
  • Ли́са, вы за́мужем?
  • Да, я за́мужем.
  • Марк, вы жена́ты?
  • Нет, я не жена́т.
*David and Lisa are married.*

3 • Меня́ зову́т О́льга Ива́новна. Я
    ру́сская. Я москви́чка. Я не
    за́мужем.
*b and c are true.*

4 • Меня́ зову́т Анн. Я америка́нка.
    Я не за́мужем.
  • Меня́ зову́т Ли́са. Я
    англича́нка. Я за́мужем.
  • Меня́ зову́т Дави́д. Я кана́дец.
    Я жена́т.
  • Меня́ зову́т Марк. Я
    австрали́ец. Я не жена́т.
*Ann – American – unmarried; Lisa –
English – married; David – Canadian –
married; Mark – Australian –
unmarried.*

**Page 19  Using the numbers 0 to 4**

**2**  *a* 2; *b* 4; *c* 3; *d* 1; *e* 0.

**3**  *a* 2; *b* 3; *c* 1; *d* 4.

**4**  *1* Она́ не америка́нка.
2 Вы англича́нин?
3 Вы жена́ты?
4 Да, он англича́нин.
5 Она́ за́мужем.
6 Вы за́мужем?
7 Она́ москви́чка.
8 Ты жена́т?

**Page 20  Put it all together**

**2**  *a* gas; *b* newspaper; *c* gesture;
*d* taxi.

**3**  *a* litre; *b* match (sport);
*c* you (formal); *d* I.

**4**  *a* whisky; *b* kilogram(me);
*c* Chekhov; *d* kiosk; *e* toilet;
*f* wine; *g* a Muscovite (m.);
*h* a Muscovite (f.).

**5**  *a* She's married; *b* He's married; *c*
She's a student; *d* He's a student;
*e* I'm not English (m.).

**Page 21  Now you're talking!**

**1**  • **Здра́вствуйте.**
• Здра́вствуйте. Как вас зову́т?
• **Меня́ зову́т Мари́я Фо́стер.
Как вас зову́т?**
• Меня́ зову́т Ива́н. Как у вас
дела́?
• **Спаси́бо, хорошо́. Вы
москви́ч?**
• Да, я москви́ч.
• **Я англича́нка.**
• О́чень рад.
• **О́чень ра́да.**

**2**  • **Меня́ зову́т Росс Смарт.**
• **Я студе́нт.**
• **Я америка́нец.**
• **Я жена́т.**

**3**  • **Вы ру́сский?**
• **Вы москви́ч?**
• **Вы студе́нт?**
• **Вы жена́ты?**

**Page 22  Quiz**

*1* b; *2* Britain; *3* b d a c; *4* Canada; *5*
*a* Yes *b* No; *6* c; *7* b; *8* Moscow; *9*
Anna; *10* Chekhov.

## Unit 3  Э́то А́нна

### Pages 24 & 25  Introducing friends and members of your family

**2**  Olga    Э́то моя́ подру́га *(a)*
        **Ле́на.** *(Lyena)*
    David   О́чень рад.
    Olga    Э́то мой друг *(b)* **Лев.**
        *(Lyev)*
    David   О́чень рад.

**3**  • Э́то мой муж **Ви́ктор.** *(Victor)*
• Э́то моя́ жена́ **Ли́дия.** *(Lydia)*

**5**  • Ле́на, у вас есть де́ти?
• Да, у меня́ есть сын.
• Лев, у вас есть сын?
• Нет, у меня́ есть дочь.
*a* Да  *b* Нет.

**6**  • Э́то моя́ подру́га.
• Как её зову́т?
• Её зову́т **Ни́на.** *(Nina)*
• О́чень рад.
• О́чень ра́да.
• А э́то мой друг.
• Как его́ зову́т?
• Его́ зову́т **Па́вел.** *(Pavel)*

### Page 26  Talking about your family

**2**  • Ни́на, у вас есть брат?
• Да, два.
• Па́вел, у вас есть сестра́?
• Да, её зову́т Со́ня.

- У вас есть де́ти?
- Нет, я не жена́т.

*c and d are true*

3  Меня́ зову́т Ве́ра. Я за́мужем.
Это мой *(b)* **муж**. Его́ зову́т
Серге́й. У меня́ есть сын. Его́
зову́т *(e)* **Никола́й**. Он не *(f)*
**жена́т**. У меня́ та́кже есть *(d)*
**дочь**. Её зову́т Ири́на. Она́ *(a)*
**за́мужем**. У неё есть дочь,
ита́к я *(c)* **ба́бушка**.

## Page 27  Giving your phone number

2  *a* 6; *b* 8; *c* 10; *d* 9; *e* 7; *f* 5.

3  Меня́ зову́т Дави́д. Мой но́мер
телефо́на **1670521** *(David)*
Меня́ зову́т Марк. Мой но́мер
телефо́на **9324186** *(Mark)*

5  *1* У вас есть де́ти?
*2* Это мой муж.
*3* Это твой брат?
*4* Это моя́ подру́га.
*5* У неё есть сын.
*6* Как его́ зову́т?

## Page 28  Put it all together

2  *a* bar; *b* lady; *c* her; *d* my; *e* park;
*f* examination.

3  car.

4  *a* diploma; *b* bus; *c* Tolstoy;
*d* expert; *e* university; *f* tram.

5  *a* This is Victor; *b* Is this your
wife? *c* I also have a son; *d* He has
a son; *e* What's her name? *f* Have
you any children?

## Page 29  Now you're talking!

1  • **Я жена́т.**
• Это ва́ша жена́?
• **Да, её зову́т Ри́та.**
• У вас есть де́ти?
• **Да у меня́ есть сын. Его́
зову́т Грег.**
• Он жена́т?
• **Он не жена́т. У него́ есть
дочь.**
• А . . . , хорошо́.

2  • **Меня́ зову́т Ли́са Па́ркер.**
• **Я студе́нтка.**
• **Я англича́нка.**
• **Я за́мужем.**
• **У меня́ есть дочь.**
• **Её зову́т Ване́сса.**

## Page 30  Quiz

*1* b; *2* informal; *3* e c a d f b; *4* your
phone number; *5* b; *6* Tolstoy; *7*
also; *8* female.

## Unit 4  Чай, пожа́луйста

## Pages 32 & 33  Ordering a drink in a bar or café

2  • Что вам уго́дно?
• Ко́фе, пожа́луйста.
*coffee.*

3  • Что вам уго́дно?
• Пи́во, пожа́луйста.
• Вино́, пожа́луйста.
• Лимона́д, пожа́луйста.
• Вода́, пожа́луйста.
• Пи́во, вино́, лимона́д и вода́?
Хорошо́.
па́па: пи́во (dad: beer); ма́ма: вино́
(mum: wine); сын: лимона́д (son:
lemonade); дочь: вода́ (daughter:
water).

**4** • Чай, пожа́луйста.
• Ко́фе, пожа́луйста.
• С са́харом?
• Нет, спаси́бо, без са́хара.
*The man has tea; the woman has coffee without sugar.*

**5** • Ко́фе, пожа́луйста, с молоко́м без са́хара.
*a with milk, no sugar.*

**6** • Чай с лимо́ном, пожа́луйста.
*lemon.*

**7** • Минера́льная вода́, пожа́луйста.
• С га́зом и́ли без га́за?
• Без га́за, пожа́луйста.
*still mineral water.*

**8** • **Пи́во, пожа́луйста**
• **Ко́фе с молоко́м, пожа́луйста**
• **Чай без са́хара, пожа́луйста**

## Page 34 Offering, accepting or refusing a drink

**2** • Что вы хоти́те?
• Пе́пси-ко́ла, пожа́луйста.
• Пе́пси-ко́ла? Хорошо́.
• Спаси́бо.
• **Пожа́луйста** *(b)*
*He asks for a coke.*

**3** • **Что ты хо́чешь** *(b)*, **Ка́тя?**
• Сок, пожа́луйста.
• А ты, Ми́ша, что хо́чешь?
• Конья́к, пожа́луйста.
*Misha orders cognac/brandy; Anna uses* **Что ты хо́чешь?** *as she knows Katya well.*

## Page 35 Using the numbers 11 to 20

**2** • Лимона́д. Двена́дцать, пожа́луйста. *12*
• Пе́пси-ко́ла. Оди́ннадцать,

пожа́луйста. *11*
• Моро́женое. Пятна́дцать, пожа́луйста. *15*

**3** *a 16; b 13; c 20; d 14; e 19.*

**4** *1* Что ты хо́чешь? *2* Конья́к, пожа́луйста. *3* Конья́к? Хорошо́. *4* Спаси́бо. *5* Пожа́луйста.

## Page 36 Put it all together

**2** *a* Fanta/fizzy orange; *b* centre; *c* champagne; *d* beetroot soup; *e* menu.

**3** object.

**4** *a* administrator; *b* telephone; *c* concert; *d* Tchaikovsky; *e* Russia; *f* St Petersburg.

**5** *a* A beer, please; *b* What would you like? *c* Tea with milk; *d* Coffee without sugar; *e* You're welcome.

## Page 37 Now you're talking!

**1** • **Что ты хо́чешь?**
• Пи́во, пожа́луйста.
• **Что вы хоти́те?**
• Пе́пси-ко́ла, пожа́луйста.
• **Здра́вствуйте. Пи́во, пе́пси-ко́ла и лимона́д, пожа́луйста.**

**2** • **Здра́вствуйте.**
• Здра́вствуйте. Что вам уго́дно?
• **Чай, пожа́луйста.**
• С са́харом?
• **С са́харом без молока́.**
• Хорошо́.
• **Спаси́бо.**
• Пожа́луйста.

**3** • **И́горь, ты хо́чешь ко́фе?**
• **С са́харом?**
• **С молоко́м?**
• **Ко́фе с молоко́м без са́хара, пожа́луйста.**

Page 38 **Quiz**

*1* a; *2* brandy; *3* b a c; *4* Coffee, a coffee, the coffee; *5* n.; *6* lemon; *7* ice cream; *8* still; *9* barman.

## Контро́льная рабо́та 1
## Pages 39–42

1
- Здра́вствуйте. Как вас зову́т?
- Меня́ зову́т **Ро́бин Мо́рсон**.
- Вы англича́нин?
- Нет, **я австрали́ец**.
- Вы жена́ты?
- Да, **я жена́т**.
- У вас есть де́ти?
- Да, **у меня́ есть сын**.
- Как его́ зову́т?
- **Его́ зову́т Кри́стофер**.

Ро́бин Мо́рсон австрали́ец. Он жена́т. У него́ есть сын. Его́ зову́т Кри́стофер.

2
- Дави́д, э́то моя́ ма́ма.
- О́чень ра́да.
- О́чень рад.
- А э́то моя́ сестра́. Её зову́т Зи́на.
- Здра́вствуй, Зи́на. Как дела́?
- Спаси́бо, хорошо́. Вы англича́нин?
- Нет, я кана́дец.

*David meets Anton's mum and sister; Anton's sister's name is Zina; she says she is well; David is from Canada.*

3 ● Что ты хо́чешь, Дави́д? Есть вино́, пи́во, чай и́ли ко́фе.
*с* лимона́д.

4 *vodka; brandy; fizzy orange; tea; tomato juice; lemonade; wine; gin; coffee; champagne; whisky; rum; milk; water; coke.*

5 *Ireland; Wales; Scotland; Italy; Spain; France; Greece; Bulgaria; Germany.*

6 *1* h; *2* g; *3* a; *4* f; *5* b; *6* d; *7* e; *8* c.

*7 a* 29; *b* 19; *c* 25; *d* 31; *e* 31.

*8 1* e; *2* d; *3* a; *4* f; *5* b; *6* c.

*9 1* c англича́нин; *2* d меня́; *3* f Её; *4* e рад; *5* a Ива́н; *6* g Как; *7* b америка́нка.
*The country is* Аме́рика.

10 Dear Elizabeth. My name's Masha. I'm a Muscovite. I'm a student in Moscow. My dad's an engineer and my mum's a guide. I have a sister. Her name's Natasha. She's a schoolgirl. I also have a grandmother. My phone number is 007 095 1670355. Goodbye. Masha.

## Unit 5 **Скажи́те, пожа́луйста, где гости́ница?**

### Pages 44 & 45 **Asking where something is and how far it is**

2
- Прости́те, пожа́луйста, где по́чта?
- Иди́те нале́во.
- Скажи́те, пожа́луйста, где метро́?
- Иди́те пря́мо.
- Скажи́те, пожа́луйста, где теа́тр?
- Иди́те пря́мо.
- Прости́те, пожа́луйста, где гости́ница?
- Иди́те напра́во.
- Скажи́те, пожа́луйста, где рестора́н?
- Иди́те пря́мо.
- Скажи́те, пожа́луйста, где музе́й?
- Иди́те нале́во.

*a* post office, left; *b* underground, straight on; *c* theatre, straight on; *d* hotel, right; *e* restaurant, straight on; *f* museum, left.

4 • Театр? Это далеко?
• Да, далеко, двадцать минут автобусом.
• Музей – далеко?
• Пять минут пешком.
• А почта? Это далеко?
• Нет, недалеко, две минуты пешком.
• Гостиница – далеко?
• Пятнадцать минут автобусом.
• Ресторан – далеко?
• Десять минут автобусом.
• А метро – далеко?
• Нет, один километр, двенадцать минут пешком.
• Один километр!! Это далеко!
a 20 by bus b 5 on foot c 2 on foot d 15 by bus e 10 by bus f 12 on foot.

## Page 46 Asking where someone lives

2 • Лиса, где вы живёте?
• Я живу в Лондоне.
• Давид, где вы живёте?
• Я живу в Ванкувере.
• Марк, где вы живёте?
• Я живу в Канберре.
• Анн, где вы живёте?
• Я живу в Нью-Йорке.
*Lisa lives in London; David lives in Vancouver; Mark lives in Canberra; Ann lives in New York.*

3 • **Лев**, ты живёшь в Москве?
• Нет, я живу в Волгограде.
• Пётр, вы живёте в Москве?
• Нет, я живу в Новгороде.
*Лев lives in Volgograd and is the one Olga knows well. Пётр lives in Novgorod.*

## Page 47 Using the numbers 21 to 199

2 • Я живу в доме тринадцать, в квартире восемьдесят девять.
a д. 13 кв. 89.

• Я живу в доме тридцать четыре, в квартире пятьдесят три.
b д. 34 кв. 53.
• Я живу в доме двадцать два, в квартире сто семьдесят восемь.
c д. 22 кв. 178.
• Я живу в доме сорок шесть, в квартире сто девяносто семь.
d д. 46 кв. 197.

## Page 48 Put it all together

1 a right; b left; c straight on.

2 a 35 kilometres; b 51 minutes; c 48 minutes; d 92 minutes; e 61 kilometres; f 83 kilometres.

3 a Петербург; b сорок; c метро; d прямо.

4 1 c; 2 a; 3 d; 4 b.

## Page 49 Now you're talking!

1 • **Скажите, пожалуйста, где метро?**
• Метро? Идите налево.
• **Это далеко?**
• Нет, пять минут пешком.
• **Где почта?**
• Почта? Идите прямо.
• **Спасибо.**

2 • Вы русский?
• **Нет, я американец. Вы русский?**
• Да, я русский.
• **Вы живёте в Санкт-Петербурге?**
• Да. Где вы живёте?
• **Я живу в Нью-Йорке**
• А . . . , хорошо.
• **Скажите, пожалуйста, где Эрмитаж?**
• Эрмитаж? Идите налево и прямо.

- **Это далеко?**
- Нет, десять минут пешком.
- **Спасибо. До свидания.**

## Page 50 Quiz

*1* right; *2* b; *3* a; *4* a (the/a) theatre (singular), b (the) theatres (plural); *5* b; *6* in a flat; *7* c.

---

## Unit 6 **Это открыто?**

### Pages 52 & 53 **Understanding what there is in town and when it's open**

2 банк *bank*; библиотека *library*; аптека *chemist's*; кино *cinema*; буфет *snackbar*; галерея *gallery*; магазин *shop*; универмаг *department store*; супермаркет *supermarket*; бассейн *swimming pool*; парк *park;* рынок *market.*

3
- Здесь есть **магазины**?
- Да, здесь есть **универмаг** и **супермаркет**.
- Где здесь **банк**?
- Здесь нет банка. Вот план города. Банк в центре.

*There is a bank in the centre.*

5 *a* Это **открыто** в субботу. *Saturday.*

*b* Это **открыто** в четверг. *Thursday.*

*c* Это **закрыто** в воскресенье. *Sunday.*

### Pages 54 & 55 **Making simple enquiries and asking for help to understand**

2
- Скажите, пожалуйста, здесь есть туалет?
- Да, здесь налево.
- Спасибо. А здесь есть телефон?

- Нет, здесь нет телефона.

*a* да; *b* нет; *c* да.

3
- Скажите, пожалуйста, где здесь почта?
- Простите, **я не знаю** (*c*). Я не москвич.

4
- Скажите, пожалуйста, где здесь почта?
- **Почта?** Идите прямо, потом направо.
- Она открыта?
- Да, сегодня открыта.

*Straight on, then right.*

*She wants to get to the post office. It's open.*

6 David    (*d*) **Скажите**, пожалуйста, где здесь библиотека?

Passer-by В центре, на улице Чехова.

David    Простите, я не понимаю. Повторите пожалуйста.

Passer-by Библиотека в (*f*) **центре**, на улице Чехова.

David    Спасибо. Она открыта во вторник?

Passer-by Да, она (*a*) **открыта**.

David    А здесь есть банк?

Passer-by Есть.

David    Он открыт?

Passer-by Нет, сегодня (*g*) **закрыт**.

David    Говорите, пожалуйста, (*e*) **медленно**.

Passer-by (*b*) **Сегодня** банк закрыт.

David    Спасибо.

Passer-by (*c*) **Пожалуйста**.

## Page 56 **Put it all together**

1 *a* Monday; *b* Tuesday to Friday; *c* 12.00 to 18.00; *d* Sunday.

Page 57 **Now you're talking!**

I • **Скажи́те, пожа́луйста, здесь есть универма́г?**
   • Да, есть, на у́лице Пу́шкина.
   • **Я не понима́ю. Повтори́те, пожа́луйста.**
   • Да, есть, на у́лице Пу́шкина.
   • **Универма́г откры́т?**
   • Да, он откры́т.
   • **Спаси́бо. Здесь есть апте́ка?**
   • Апте́ка? Иди́те напра́во, пото́м пря́мо.
   • **Говори́те, пожа́луйста, ме́дленно.**
   • Апте́ка – напра́во, пото́м пря́мо.
   • **Напра́во, пото́м пря́мо. Она́ откры́та?**
   • Да, она́ откры́та.
   • **Спаси́бо.**
   • Пожа́луйста.

2 • **Вот план го́рода.**
   • **Магази́ны в це́нтре.**
   • **Здесь есть ры́нок в четве́рг.**
   • **По́чта закры́та в воскресе́нье.**
   • **Здесь нет ба́нка.**

Page 58 **Quiz**

*1* in the centre; 2 closed; 3 a map of the town; 4 b; 5 c a b; 6 Sunday; 7 a.

Unit 7 **Ско́лько сто́ит?**

Pages 60 & 61 **Using the numbers above 200 and understanding prices**

2 *a* 5р 22к; *b* 41р 15к; *c* 1 363р.

3 *a* 7р 60к; *b* 107р 50к; *c* 1 196р 75к.

5 откры́тка *postcard*; почто́вая ма́рка *postage stamp*; аспири́н

*aspirin*; фотоаппара́т *camera*; шампа́нское *champagne*; сувени́ры *souvenirs*.

6 • Ско́лько сто́ит **аспири́н?**
*(aspirin)*
   • **Пятьдеся́т копе́ек.**
*(50 kopecks)*

7 • Здра́вствуйте. У вас есть **фотоаппара́т?**
   • Да, вот фотоаппара́ты.
   • Ско́лько сто́ят?
   • **Пятьсо́т рубле́й.**
*(500 roubles)*
   • Спаси́бо. Да́йте, пожа́луйста, оди́н. Скажи́те, пожа́луйста, ско́лько сто́ит **шампа́нское?**
   • **Со́рок рубле́й пятьдеся́т копе́ек.**
*(40 roubles 50 kopeks)*
шампа́нское 40 roubles 50 kopecks; фотоаппара́т 500 roubles.

8 • Здра́вствуйте. Ско́лько сто́ят **откры́тки?**
   • **Два́дцать копе́ек.**
*(20 kopecks)*
   • Да́йте, пожа́луйста, **три.** *(3)*
   • Ско́лько сто́ит **ма́рка в Аме́рику?**
   • **Се́мьдесят пять копе́ек.**
*(75 kopecks)*
*postcard costs 20 kopecks; she buys 3; stamp for America costs 75 kopecks.*

Pages 62 & 63 **Asking for items in a shop or market**

2 • Здра́вствуйте. У вас есть сувени́ры?
   • Да. Что вы хоти́те?
   • Я не зна́ю.
   • Вот матрёшка и́ли ша́пка.
   • Мо́жно посмотре́ть?
   • Мо́жно. Вот, пожа́луйста.
   • Ско́лько сто́ит ша́пка?
   • Шестьсо́т рубле́й.
   • Хорошо́. А ско́лько сто́ит **матрёшка?**

- Пятьдеся́т три рубля́. Вы
  хоти́те?
- Да, пожа́луйста.
- Это всё?
- Да, э́то всё.
- Плати́те в ка́ссу.
*set of Russian dolls.*

3
- Матрёшка, **пятьдеся́т три
  рубля́.**
  - Вот **чек** и сда́ча.
  - Спаси́бо.
  - Пожа́луйста.
*53 roubles; a receipt.*

4 У вас есть ло́жки? Мо́жно
  посмотре́ть?
  У вас есть во́дка? Мо́жно
  посмотре́ть?
  У вас есть икра́? Мо́жно
  посмотре́ть?
  У вас есть матрёшка? Мо́жно
  посмотре́ть?
  У вас есть ша́пка? Мо́жно
  посмотре́ть?

5 *a* (bread); *b* (apples); *c*
  (tomatoes); *d* (cheese); *e* (milk).

6
- Ско́лько сто́ят **я́блоки?**
- Шесть рубле́й килогра́мм.
- Да́йте мне, пожа́луйста,
  килогра́мм.
- Что ещё?
- **Помидо́ры** – полкило́,
  пожа́луйста.
- Это всё?
- Да, э́то всё.
- Де́сять рубле́й пятьдеся́т
  копе́ек.
- Спаси́бо.
- Пожа́луйста.
- **Молоко́**, пожа́луйста, – паке́т.
- Что ещё?
- **Сыр**, пожа́луйста, – две́сти
  пятьдеся́т грамм.
- Что ещё?
- Это всё, спаси́бо.
*1 b* я́блоки; *2 c* помидо́ры; *3 e*

молоко́; *4 d* сыр.
*She forgets to buy bread – a* хлеб.

## Page 64 **Put it all together**

1 *a* 1 917; *b* 7 496; *c* 22 583; *d* 500
  155

2 *a* May I have a look? *b* Could you
  give me . . . ? *c* That's all; *d* How
  much is it? *e* Have you got . . . ?
  *f* Anything else? *g* How much are
  they?

3 *1* У вас есть помидо́ры? *2* Да,
  есть. *3* Ско́лько сто́ят? *4* Семь
  рубле́й – килогра́мм. *5* Да́йте,
  пожа́луйста, полкило́.

4 150g. cheese; 2 loaves; 4
  tomatoes; 1 litre mineral water;
  half kg. apples.

## Page 65 **Now you're talking!**

1
- **Здра́вствуйте. У вас есть
  сувени́ры?**
- Да. Что вы хоти́те?
- **Я не зна́ю.**
- Вот, пожа́луйста, ло́жки и́ли
  матрёшка.
- **Мо́жно посмотре́ть?**
- Мо́жно. Вот, пожа́луйста.
- **Ско́лько сто́ят ло́жки?**
- Два́дцать пять рубле́й.
- **(А) ско́лько сто́ит
  матрёшка?**
- Пятьдеся́т рубле́й.
- **Да́йте, пожа́луйста, ло́жки.**
- Хорошо́. Это всё?
- **Да, э́то всё, спаси́бо.**
- Плати́те в ка́ссу два́дцать пять
  рубле́й.

2
- **Ло́жки. Два́дцать пять
  рубле́й.**
- Пожа́луйста, чек.
- **Спаси́бо.**
- Пожа́луйста.

3 • **Пожа́луйста, чек** or **Вот чек.**
 • Пожа́луйста, ло́жки.
 • **Спаси́бо.**
 • Пожа́луйста.

## Page 66 **Quiz**

*1* b; *2* b; *3* 100; *4* a large department store in Moscow; *5* to pay at the cash desk; *6* b; *7* c

## Контро́льная рабо́та 2
Pages 67–70

1 • Прости́те, пожа́луйста, здесь есть **банк?**
 • Иди́те пря́мо. Э́то у́лица Го́голя. Вот нале́во – банк.
 • Спаси́бо.
 • Пожа́луйста.
*a* bank *(box 1)*.

 • Скажи́те, пожа́луйста, где **рестора́н** 'Кали́нка'?
 • Иди́те пря́мо, напра́во, пото́м нале́во. Э́то у́лица Сре́тенка. Вот напра́во – рестора́н 'Кали́нка'.
 • Повтори́те, пожа́луйста.
 • Иди́те пря́мо, напра́во, пото́м нале́во. Э́то у́лица Сре́тенка. Вот напра́во – рестора́н 'Кали́нка'.
*b* Kalinka restaurant *(box 3)*.

 • Скажи́те, пожа́луйста, где здесь **по́чта?**
 • По́чта? Иди́те пря́мо, пото́м напра́во. Э́то Проспе́кт Ми́ра. Вот напра́во – по́чта.
 • Прости́те, я не понима́ю. Говори́те, пожа́луйста, ме́дленно.
 • А . . . , хорошо́. Иди́те пря́мо, пото́м напра́во. Э́то Проспе́кт Ми́ра. Вот напра́во – по́чта.
*c* post office *(box 2)*.

2 • Прости́те, пожа́луйста, банк откры́т?
 • Нет, сего́дня **закры́т.**
*a* closed.

 • Скажи́те, пожа́луйста, рестора́н 'Кали́нка' откры́т?
 • Да, он **откры́т.**
*b* open.

 • Скажи́те, пожа́луйста, по́чта откры́та?
 • Да, она́ **откры́та.**
*c* open.

3 во́дка – ли́тр **40**р.
 молоко́ – паке́т **4**р. **50**к.
 хлеб – бато́н **3**р. **20**к.
 сыр – 300г **2**р. **20**к.
 помидо́ры – полкило́ **7**р. **50**к.

4 *a* Moscow; *b* 52; *c* Ivanov.

5 *a* суббо́та; *b* чек; *c* кварти́ра; *d* ша́пка.

6 *1* b; *2* e; *3* c; *4* a; *5* d.

7 *1* b; *2* a; *3* e; *4* c; *5* d.

8 *a* нет; *b* да; *c* нет; *d* да; *e* да; *f* нет; *g* да.

## Unit 8 **У вас есть свобо́дный но́мер?**

### Page 72 **Checking in at reception**

2 • Здра́вствуйте. Меня́ зову́т Бен Бра́ун. Я заказа́л **двухме́стный но́мер с ду́шем.**
 • Ваш па́спорт, пожа́луйста.
 • Вот мой па́спорт.
*double room with a shower*

 • Здра́вствуйте. Я заказа́ла **одноме́стный но́мер с ду́шем.**

- Ва́ша фами́лия, пожа́луйста.
- Смит.

*single room with a shower.*

- Здра́вствуйте.
- Здра́вствуйте. Я заказа́ла **но́мер люкс**.
- Ва́ша фами́лия, пожа́луйста.
- А́ндерсон.
- А́ндерсон. Вот . . . но́мер три́ста пять **с ва́нной и с ду́шем**.

*luxury room with a bath and shower.*

## Page 73 **Asking if there's a room free**

2 • Здра́вствуйте. У вас есть свобо́дный но́мер?
- На ско́лько челове́к?
- На **два**.
- На ско́лько дней?
- На **три дня**.
- Како́й но́мер вы хоти́те?
- Но́мер **с ва́нной**, пожа́луйста.
- Ва́ша фами́лия, пожа́луйста.
- **Каре́нин**.

фами́лия: Каре́нин; коли́чество челове́к: два; коли́чество дней: три дня; но́мер: с ва́нной.

- Здра́вствуйте. У вас есть свобо́дный но́мер?
- Како́й но́мер вы хоти́те?
- **С ду́шем**, пожа́луйста.
- На ско́лько дней?
- На **семь дней**.
- И на ско́лько челове́к?
- На **два**.
- Хорошо́. Ва́ша фами́лия, пожа́луйста.
- **Петро́ва**.
- Ваш па́спорт, пожа́луйста.
- Вот мой па́спорт.

фами́лия: Петро́ва; коли́чество челове́к: два; коли́чество дней: семь дней; но́мер: с ду́шем.

## Page 74 **Asking which floor something is on**

2 *a* 7th; *b* 11th; *c* 5th; *d* 8th.

3 • Ва́ша фами́лия, пожа́луйста.
- **Бра́ун**.
- Ваш но́мер **на оди́ннадцатом этаже́**.

- Ва́ша фами́лия, пожа́луйста.
- **Смит**.
- Вы **на седьмо́м этаже́**.

- Ва́ша фами́лия, пожа́луйста.
- **А́ндерсон**.
- Но́мер три́дцать, **на пе́рвом этаже́**.

*1* b; *2* a; *3* c.

## Page 75 **Making requests**

2 • Мо́жно оплати́ть креди́тной ка́ртой?
- Мо́жно.
- Мо́жно заказа́ть такси́?
- Стоя́нка такси́ нале́во, недалеко́.

*a* by credit card; *b* on the left, not far.

- Мо́жно посмотре́ть но́мер?
- Да, он на второ́м этаже́.
- Где лифт?
- Здесь, напра́во.

*c* 1st (literally 2nd in English); *d* on the right.

- Мо́жно пообе́дать в гости́нице?
- Да, рестора́н откры́т.

*e* Yes.

## Page 76 **Put it all together**

1 *1* У вас есть свобо́дный но́мер?
*2* Да, есть. На ско́лько дней?
*3* На три дня.
*4* И на ско́лько челове́к?

5 На два.
6 Есть двухме́стный но́мер на седьмо́м этаже́.
7 Мо́жно посмотре́ть но́мер?
8 Мо́жно. Вот ключ.

2 *1* d; *2* a; *3* b; *4* c; *5* e.

3 *1* b; *2* e; *3* a; *4* d; *5* c.

## Page 77 Now you're talking!

1 • Здра́вствуйте. У вас есть свобо́дный но́мер?
• Одноме́стный и́ли двухме́стный но́мер?
• Одноме́стный с ду́шем, пожа́луйста.
• На ско́лько дней?
• На два дня.
• Хорошо́. Есть свобо́дный но́мер на пя́том этаже́.
• Мо́жно посмотре́ть?
• Мо́жно. Вот ключ.

2 • Ва́ша фами́лия, пожа́луйста.
• Петро́ва.
• Ваш па́спорт, пожа́луйста.
• Вот мой па́спорт.
• Спаси́бо.
• Мо́жно пообе́дать в гости́нице?
• Да, рестора́н откры́т.
• Рестора́н на како́м этаже́?
• На тре́тьем этаже́.
• Мо́жно оплати́ть креди́тной ка́ртой?
• Да, мо́жно.
• Спаси́бо.
• Пожа́луйста.

## Page 78 Quiz

*1* a; *2* passport; *3* ground floor; *4* manager; *5* registration form; *6* lift; *7* surname.

# Unit 9 Когда́ отхо́дит?

## Page 80 Asking about public transport

2 • Скажи́те, пожа́луйста, како́й трамва́й идёт до метро́?
• Трамва́й но́мер се́мьдесят три.
*a* tram; *73*; the Metro (underground).

• Прости́те, пожа́луйста, како́й тролле́йбус идёт до по́чты?
• Тролле́йбус но́мер три.
*b* trolleybus; *3*; post office.

• Скажи́те, пожа́луйста, есть авто́бус до Эрмита́жа?
• Есть. Авто́бус но́мер два́дцать два. Вот напра́во – остано́вка.
*c* bus; *22*; the Hermitage (museum).

3 Есть авто́бус до аэропо́рта?
Како́й тролле́йбус идёт до вокза́ла?
Како́й трамва́й идёт до у́лицы Пу́шкина?

## Page 81 Finding out train times

2 *a* 21.15; *b* 17.21; *c* 22.43; *d* 06.35.

3 • Скажи́те, пожа́луйста, когда́ отхо́дит по́езд до Оде́ссы?
• В 03.00.
• А когда́ я бу́ду в Оде́ссе?
• В 23.30.
*depart 03.00; arrive 23.30.*

• Когда́ отхо́дит сле́дующий по́езд до Я́лты?
• В 02.50.
• А в кото́ром часу́ я бу́ду в Я́лте?
• В 22.45.
*depart 02.50; arrive 22.45.*

- Прости́те, пожа́луйста, в
  кото́ром часу́ отхо́дит
  сле́дующий по́езд до Ки́ева?
- В **08.05**.
- А когда́ я бу́ду в Ки́еве?
- В **21.58**.

*depart 08.05; arrive 21.58.*

## Page 82 **Buying train tickets**

2
- Оди́н биле́т до Москвы́,
  пожа́луйста.
- В оди́н коне́ц и́ли туда́ и
  обра́тно?
- **В оди́н коне́ц**, пожа́луйста.

- Да́йте мне, пожа́луйста, два
  биле́та до Но́вгорода.
- В оди́н коне́ц и́ли туда́ и
  обра́тно?
- **В оди́н коне́ц**, пожа́луйста.
- Пожа́луйста, сто во́семьдесят
  рубле́й.

- Да́йте мне, пожа́луйста, биле́т
  до Оде́ссы.
- Биле́т в оди́н коне́ц?
- Нет, **биле́т туда́ и обра́тно**,
  пожа́луйста.

- Да́йте, пожа́луйста, **биле́т в
  оди́н коне́ц** до Я́лты.
- Девяно́сто пять рубле́й.

3
- Прости́те, пожа́луйста, с како́й
  платфо́рмы отхо́дит по́езд до
  **Но́вгорода**?
- С платфо́рмы но́мер **три**.

*a Novgorod; platform 3.*

- Скажи́те, пожа́луйста, с како́й
  платфо́рмы отхо́дит
  сле́дующий по́езд до **Я́лты**?
- С платфо́рмы но́мер
  **оди́ннадцать**.

*b Yalta; platform 11.*

- Прости́те, пожа́луйста, с како́й
  платфо́рмы отхо́дит по́езд до
  **Москвы́**?

- С платфо́рмы но́мер **четы́ре**.

*c Moscow; platform 4*

- С како́й платфо́рмы отхо́дит
  сле́дующий по́езд до
  **Оде́ссы**?
- С платфо́рмы но́мер **семь**.

*d Odessa; platform 7*

## Page 83 **Finding your way around the Metro**

2
- Прости́те, пожа́луйста, на́до
  купи́ть биле́т?
- Нет. В метро́ на́до купи́ть
  жето́н. Вот напра́во — ка́сса.

- Скажи́те, пожа́луйста, где
  ста́нция Ки́евская?
- Вот схе́ма метро́ и вот —
  Ки́евская.
- Спаси́бо. На́до де́лать
  переса́дку?
- Нет, не на́до.

- Скажи́те мне, пожа́луйста,
  когда́ на́до выходи́ть?
- Сле́дующая ста́нция Ки́евская.

*a Нет; b Нет; c Да.*

3
- **1** Ста́нция **Пло́щадь
  Револю́ции** . . .
  Осторо́жно, две́ри
  закрыва́ются. Сле́дующая
  ста́нция Арба́тская.

- **2** Ста́нция **Арба́тская** . . .
  Осторо́жно, две́ри
  закрыва́ются. Сле́дующая
  ста́нция Смоле́нская

- **3** Ста́нция **Смоле́нская** . . .
  Осторо́жно, две́ри
  закрыва́ются. Сле́дующая
  ста́нция Ки́евская.

- **4** Ста́нция **Ки́евская** . . .
  Осторо́жно, две́ри

закрыва́ются. Сле́дующая
ста́нция Парк Побе́ды.

## Page 84 **Put it all together**

1   *1* c; *2* e; *3* a; *4* d; *5* b.

2   *a* в час; *b* в трина́дцать часо́в; *c* в
четы́ре часа́; *d* в шестна́дцать
часо́в; *e* в семь часо́в де́сять
мину́т;
*f* в девятна́дцать часо́в де́сять
мину́т.

3   *1* d; *2* e; *3* b; *4* a; *5* c.

4   *a* авто́бус; *b* по́езд; *c*
тролле́йбус; *d* трамва́й

## Page 85 **Now you're talking!**

1   • **Это далеко́?**
    • Нет, де́сять мину́т
    тролле́йбусом.
    • **Како́й тролле́йбус?**
    • Тролле́йбус но́мер два́дцать
    шесть.
    • **Где остано́вка?**
    • Вот нале́во – остано́вка.

2   • **Скажи́те, пожа́луйста, где
    ста́нция Ки́евская?**
    • Вот схе́ма метро́ и вот –
    Ки́евская.
    • **На́до де́лать переса́дку?**
    • Нет, не на́до.

3   • **Биле́т в оди́н коне́ц до
    Санкт-Петербу́рга,
    пожа́луйста.**
    • Девяно́сто рубле́й.
    • **Когда́ отхо́дит сле́дующий
    по́езд?**
    • В два́дцать два часа́.
    • **С како́й платфо́рмы
    отхо́дит по́езд?**
    • С платфо́рмы но́мер
    двена́дцать.

## Page 86 **Quiz**

*1* Metro token; *2* aeroplane; *3* for
information; *4* a railway station  *b*
Metro station; *5* b; *6* return; *7*
change trains.

## Unit 10 **Прия́тного
аппети́та!**

### Page 90 **Asking what's available**

2   • Молодо́й челове́к! Да́йте,
    пожа́луйста, **меню́**.
    • Пожа́луйста, меню́.
*The menu.*

3   • Каки́е заку́ски у вас есть?
    • Есть **колбаса́, винегре́т,
    грибы́ в смета́не, сарди́ны
    в ма́сле**.
    • У вас есть **чёрная икра́**?
    • Нет, то́лько **кра́сная икра́**.
*1* d; *2* f; *3* e; *4* c; *5* b; *6* a.
*There is no black caviar – b* чёрная
икра́

4   • А что у вас есть сего́дня на
    пе́рвое?
    • Пожа́луйста, есть щи, борщ и
    бульо́н.
    • У вас есть **уха́**?
    • Есть.
*Fish soup.*

5   • Сего́дня на второ́е есть
    шашлы́к, бефстро́ганов, ку́рица
    с ри́сом, карп с гриба́ми.
*a* да; *b* нет; *c* нет; *d* да.

### Page 91 **Ordering a meal**

2   • Де́вушка!
    • Слу́шаю вас.
    • Да́йте, пожа́луйста, **винегре́т**.
    • Хорошо́. А вы хоти́те суп?
    • Спаси́бо, нет. Что вы
    рекоменду́ете на второ́е?

- **Ку́рицу с ри́сом.**
- Да́йте мне, пожа́луйста, ку́рицу.
- А на десе́рт?
- **Моро́женое**, пожа́луйста.

3 • Что вы бу́дете пить?
- **Во́дку**, пожа́луйста.
*Vodka.*

4 • Де́вушка! Счёт, пожа́луйста.
- **Две́сти се́мьдесят пять рубле́й.**
*b* 275 рубле́й.

## Pages 92 & 93 **Saying what you like and don't like**

2 • Мне нра́вится **ры́ба.** Тебе́ нра́вится карп, Ми́ша?
- Да, мне нра́вится **карп.**
- Что тебе́ нра́вится, Пётр?
- Мне нра́вится **бефстро́ганов.**
- А Ната́ша . . . ?
- Мне нра́вится **бифште́кс.**
*a* ма́ма; *b* дочь (Ната́ша); *c* сын (Пётр); *d* па́па (Ми́ша).

3 **Мне нра́вится икра́.**
**Мне нра́вятся блины́.**
**Мне нра́вится кра́сное вино́.**
**Мне нра́вятся холо́дные заку́ски.**

5 • Слу́шаю вас.
- Да́йте, пожа́луйста, **грибы́ в смета́не.** Мне о́чень нра́вятся.
- Хорошо́.
*Mushrooms in sour cream.*

6 • Да́йте мне, пожа́луйста, **сала́т.**
- Пётр, что ты хо́чешь?
- Икру́, пожа́луйста.
- Тебе́ бо́льше нра́вится кра́сная и́ли **чёрная икра́?**
- Чёрная, коне́чно.

7 • Ната́ша, что ты хо́чешь?
- Спаси́бо, ничего́. Мне не нра́вятся холо́дные заку́ски.
*She doesn't like cold starters.*

8 Метрдоте́ль (*b*) **Всё** норма́льно?
Па́па (*d*) **Да**, спаси́бо.
Метрдоте́ль Тебе́ (*a*) **нра́вится** десе́рт?
Пётр Да, э́то о́чень (*c*) **вку́сно.**

## Page 94 **Put it all together**

1 *a* with jam; *b* in tomato sauce; *c* fried; *d* in butter; *e* garnished with vegetables; *f* with mushrooms; *g* tasty.

2 заку́ски – *d* икра́, *j* винегре́т
пе́рвые блю́да – *g* борщ, *i* щи
вторы́е блю́да – *b* шашлы́к
*c* ку́рица *e* щука
десе́рт – *a* торт *f* я́блоки *h* моро́женое

3 *a* **Мне нра́вится колбаса́**
*b* **Мне нра́вятся помидо́ры**
*c* **Мне нра́вятся ру́сские заку́ски**
*To say you don't like them, add* **не**
*after* **Мне.**

4 *1* Молодо́й челове́к! *2* Слу́шаю вас. *3* Что вы рекоменду́ете на десе́рт? *4* Торт с фру́ктами. Э́то о́чень вку́сно. *5* Хорошо́. Да́йте мне, пожа́луйста, торт.

## Page 95 **Now you're talking!**

1 • **Молодо́й челове́к! Да́йте, пожа́луйста, меню́.**
- Вот меню́.
- **Спаси́бо.**
- Пожа́луйста.

2 • Слу́шаю вас.
- **Сарди́ны в ма́сле, пожа́луйста.**

- А на пе́рвое?
- **Борщ, пожа́луйста.**
- Хорошо́, а на второ́е?
- **Мне нра́вится ры́ба. Что вы рекоменду́ете?**
- Сего́дня есть карп с гриба́ми. Э́то о́чень вку́сно.
- **Карп с гриба́ми, пожа́луйста.**
- Что вы бу́дете пить?
- **Да́йте мне пожа́луйста, бе́лое вино́.**

3 • Всё норма́льно? Вам нра́вится карп?
- **Мне о́чень нра́вится.**
- Что вы бу́дете на десе́рт?
- **Спаси́бо, ничего́. Мне не нра́вится десе́рт.**

Page 96 **Quiz**

*1* menu; *2* b; *3* d c a b; *4* give your order; *5* tea (чай); *6* b; *7* c.

## Контро́льная рабо́та 3
Pages 97–100

*1* • Когда́ отхо́дит по́езд но́мер трина́дцать?
• **В семь часо́в три́дцать мину́т.**
*a* 07.30.

• В кото́ром часу́ отхо́дит по́езд но́мер шесть?
• **В два́дцать три часа́ пятьдеся́т мину́т.**
*b* 23.50.

• В кото́ром часу́ отхо́дит сле́дующий по́езд до Ми́нска?
• По́езд но́мер два́дцать отхо́дит **в де́сять часо́в де́сять мину́т.**
*c* 10.10.

• Когда́ отхо́дит по́езд до Волгогра́да?
• По́езд но́мер во́семь отхо́дит **в два́дцать оди́н час пятна́дцать мину́т.**
*d* 21.15.

*2* *b* Скажи́те, пожа́луйста, здесь есть буфе́т?

*3* *left.*

*4* *a* квас; лимона́д; минера́льная вода́; молоко́; пе́пси-ко́ла; тома́тный сок; фа́нта
*b* чай с лимо́ном.

*5* *a* **Здра́вствуйте. Я англича́нин** (m.) / **англича́нка** (f.).
*b* **Вы ру́сский? Где вы живёте?**
*c* **Мне о́чень нра́вится Москва́.**

*6* • Скажи́те, пожа́луйста, где гости́ница 'Пра́га'?
• Гости́ница 'Пра́га'? Иди́те напра́во. Э́то у́лица Ду́рова. Иди́те пря́мо, пото́м нале́во. Э́то Мане́жная пло́щадь и вот нале́во – гости́ница 'Пра́га'.
*Go right. This is Durova Street. Go straight on, then left. This is Manezhnaya Square and the Hotel Prague is to your left.*

*7* *c* Я заказа́ла двухме́стный но́мер с ду́шем.

*8* *3rd floor.*

*9* АДМИНИСТРА́ТОР *manager*; ТУАЛЕ́Т *toilet*; РЕСТОРА́Н *restaurant*; ЛИФТ *lift*; ТЕЛЕФО́Н *telephone*; СА́УНА *sauna*; БАР *bar*; СУВЕНИ́РЫ *souvenirs*.

**10** Я заказа́л(а) одноме́стный но́мер с ва́нной на три дня. Мо́жно пообе́дать в гости́нице? Рестора́н на како́м этаже́? Мо́жно оплати́ть креди́тной ка́ртой?

**11** • Да́йте мне, пожа́луйста:
gribы́ в смета́не
бульо́н с пирожка́ми
шашлы́к
блины́ с варе́ньем
квас

**12** 1 рубль / банк
2 бассе́йн / вода́
3 бар / кафе́
4 ма́рка / откры́тка
5 кварти́ра / дом
6 ка́сса / чек
7 Эрмита́ж / музе́й
8 откры́т / закры́т

**13**

| а | н | ц | у | е | т | й | у | в | т | с | в | а | р | д | з | а |
|---|---|---|---|---|---|---|---|---|---|---|---|---|---|---|---|---|
| я | к | а | е | н | г | ш | щ | л | з | х | ф | ы | в | а | п | р |
| и | о | л | р | д | б | э | я | ч | и | с | м | и | т | б | ю | ж |
| н | ь | ь | ё | о | ц | р | т | н | е | ц | у | к | е | н | г | ш |
| а | а | в | ы | ф | т | л | о | р | п | а | п | т | е | к | а |   |
| д | н | с | ч | я | э | с | у | в | т | с | в | о | р | д | з | а |
| и | т | и | м | с | п | и | е | т | б | о | т | ч | ю | ё | й | ц |
| в | е | к | у | а | т | й | у | р | т | с | в | т | р | е | н | г |
| с | н | а | с | е | е | ф | о | к | о | р | а | л | д | э | ж |   |
| о | т | и | а | м | и | т | р | в | а | х | щ | г | п | т | о | я |
| д | б | а | ф | е | т | ы | щ | э | ы | ф | т | м | н | у | я | г |
| о | в | п | х | д | т | й | и | л | ю | щ | е | о | м | ш | а | е |
| в | ё | п | х | о | т | ы | у | р | н | э | д | к | и | л | х | ш |

# Grammar

Grammar is the term used to describe the patterns of a language. Russian grammar is complex with numerous sets of endings for nouns and adjectives which take time to get used to. Below is a very brief summary of some essential grammar points.

1 **Nouns** (words for people, things, places, concepts) have a gender: masculine (m.), feminine (f.) or neuter (n.).

**nouns in the singular** (one only)

*a* Masculine nouns usually end in a consonant, or **й**:
лимона́**д**, ча**й**

*b* Feminine nouns usually end in **-a** or **-я**:
вод**а́**, тёт**я**

*c* Neuter nouns usually end in **-o** or **-e**:
вин**о́**, моро́жено**е**

There are no articles (words for 'the, a/an') in Russian, so **чай** can mean 'tea', 'a tea' or 'the tea'.

**nouns in the plural** (more than one)

Nouns change their endings for the plural.

One of the most common endings is **ы**:

| | |
|---|---|
| Где гости́ница? | Where is the hotel? (singular) |
| Где гости́ниц**ы**?' | Where are the hotels? (plural) |

2 Adjectives (words which describe) have to 'agree' with whatever they describe in gender, number and case:

| | |
|---|---|
| бифште́кс **натура́льный** (m.) | beefsteak – grilled |
| **кра́сная** икра́ (f.) | red caviar |
| **бе́лое** вино́ (n.) | white wine |
| **ру́сские** блины́ (plural) | Russian pancakes |
| на **второ́м** этаже́ | on the 1st |
| (after prepositions) | (literally 2nd) floor |

**3** **Pronouns** (words used instead of nouns) also change according to their case/function in a sentence.

The subject (nominative) pronouns are:

| | | | |
|---|---|---|---|
| **я** | I | **мы** | we |
| **ты** | you | **вы** | you |
| **он** | he/it | **они** | they |
| **она́** | she/it | | |
| **оно́** | it | | |

There are two words for 'you' in Russian:

**ты**  a friend, member of the family, young person

**вы**  (often written **Вы**) someone you don't know well, someone older, more than one person

Examples of pronouns used in other cases include:

**меня́** (accusative): **Меня́** зову́т А́нна.  They call me Anna.

**мне** (dative): Да́йте **мне** ключ.  Give (to) me the key.

**4** **Cases** The endings of nouns, adjectives and pronouns change, depending on their case/function in a sentence. Russian has six cases.

I **Nominative** – used for the subject of a sentence and the form found in dictionaries:

**Студе́нт** жена́т.  The student is married.

2 **Accusative** – used for the direct object of a sentence:

Да́йте мне **ключ.**  Give me the key.

and after some prepositions:

Плати́те **в ка́ссу.**  Pay at the cash-desk.

3 **Genitive** – used after many prepositions and for 'possession' ('of'):

Есть авто́бус **до вокза́ла?**  Is there a bus to the station?

It is also used after '**нет**' (there isn't/aren't):

Здесь **нет ба́нка**.  There isn't a bank here.

4 **Dative** – used after certain prepositions and for the indirect object after verbs e.g. 'да́ть' (to give):

Да́йте **мне** ло́жки. Give (to) me the spoons.

5 **Instrumental** – used to express 'by', and after some prepositions, particularly '**с**' (with):

Пять минут **автобусом**.　　Five minutes by bus.
Чай **с сахаром**.　　Tea with sugar.

6 **Prepositional** – used only after certain prepositions:
Я живу **в Москве**.　　I live in Moscow.

5 **Verbs** (words for doing or being) change their endings according to who or what is the subject:

**Я живу** в Москве.　　I live in Moscow.
**Вы живёте** в Москве.　　You live in Moscow.

The form found in the dictionary is called the **infinitive**, usually ending in **-ть** in Russian:
**говорить** 'to' talk/speak; **быть** 'to' be; **знать** 'to' know.

The infinitive can be used after words such as **Можно / Надо**:
**Можно посмотреть?**　　Can I/we have a look?
Когда **надо выходить?**　　When do I have to get off?

6 There are no words for 'am, is, are' in Russian:

Она студентка.　　She is a student.
Где Анна?　　Where's Anna?

7 To say something negative, add **не**:

Она **не** студентка.　　She is not a student.
Я **не** знаю.　　I don't know.

8 **Prepositions** (words like **в**, 'in', **с** 'with', **до** 'to') take a particular case. Some can take two different cases·depending on their meaning/function:

**В субботу** он заказал бифштекс **в ресторане**.
On Saturday he ordered a steak in the restaurant.
**В субботу** is in the accusative; **в ресторане** is in the prepositional.

# Russian–English glossary

This glossary contains only those words and phrases, and their meanings, as they occur in Talk Russian. Parts of verbs are also given in the form in which they occur, usually followed by the infinitive in brackets.

## Аа

а *but, and*
а́вия *air mail*
австрали́ец *Australian*
Австра́лия *Australia*
авто́бус *bus*:
  авто́бусом *by bus*
автомоби́ль (m.) *car*
администра́тор
  *administrator, manager*
Аме́рика *America*:
  в Аме́рику *to America*
америка́нец *American (m.)*
америка́нка *American (f.)*
англича́нин *English (m.)*
англича́нка *English (f.)*
А́нглия *England*
анке́та *registration form*
аппети́т *appetite*:
  Прия́тного аппети́та!
  *Enjoy your meal!*
апте́ка *chemist*
аспири́н *aspirin*
ата́ка *attack*
а́том *atom*
аэропо́рт *airport*

## Бб

ба́бушка *grandmother*
банк *bank*
бар *bar*
барме́н *barman*
бассе́йн *swimming pool*
бато́н *loaf*
без *without*
бе́лое *white*
Белору́ссия *Belarus*
бефстро́ганов *beef
  Stroganoff*

библиоте́ка *library*
биле́т *ticket*
бифште́кс *beefsteak*:
  бифште́кс натура́льный
  *grilled beefsteak*
блины́ *pancakes*
блю́да *dishes, courses*
Болга́рия *Bulgaria*
бо́льше *more, bigger*:
  мне бо́льше нра́вится
  *I prefer*
борщ *beetroot soup*
бра́во *bravo, well done*
брат *brother*
брита́нец *British (m.)*
Брита́ния *Britain*
(вы) бу́дете (быть)
  *(you) will be*
(я) бу́ду (быть) *(I )will be*
бульва́р *boulevard*
бульо́н *clear soup*
буфе́т *snackbar, buffet*
бюро́ *office, desk*:
  спра́вочное бюро́
  *enquiry desk, information
  office*

## Вв

в, во *in, into*:
  в оди́н коне́ц *single
  (ticket)*
вам *(to) you (formal)*:
  вам нра́вится? *do you
  like?*
Ванку́вер *Vancouver*
ва́нна *bath*:
  с ва́нной *with a bath*
варе́нье *jam*:
  с варе́ньем *with jam*

вас *you (formal)*:
  как вас зову́т?
  *what's your name?* у вас
  есть? *have you got?*
ваш (m.) ва́ша (f.)
  ва́ше (n.) *your (formal)*
винегре́т *vegetable salad*
вино́ *wine*
ви́ски *whisky*
вку́сно *tasty*
вода́ *water*
во́дка *vodka*
вокза́л *station*
Волгогра́д *Volgograd*
воскресе́нье *Sunday*
вот *here, here is/are*
всё *all, everything*
вто́рник *Tuesday*
второ́й (m.) втора́я (f.)
второ́е (n.) *second*:
  второ́е *second (main)
  course*;
  вторы́е блю́да *second
  courses*; на второ́м
  этаже́ *on the 2nd floor*
вы *you (formal)*
выходи́ть *to get off*
выходно́й день (m)
  *closing day, day off*

## Гг

газ *gas*:
  без га́за *still (water)*
  с га́зом *sparkling (water)*
газе́та *newspaper*
галере́я *gallery*
гарни́р *garnish*:
  с гарни́ром *garnished,
  with vegetables*

где *where*
Герма́ния *Germany*
гид *guide*
говори́те (говори́ть)
  *speak*
го́род *town*
горя́чий *hot:*
  горя́чие блю́да *hot*
  *dishes*
гости́ница *hotel*
грамм *gram(me)*
Гре́ция *Greece*
грибы́ *mushrooms:*
  с гриба́ми *with*
  *mushrooms*
Гру́зия *Georgia*
гуля́ш *goulash*
ГУМ *GUM, Moscow*
  *department store*

## Дд

да *yes*
да́йте (дава́ть) *give*
далеко́ *far*
да́ма *lady*
два (m./n.), две (f.) *two*
две́ри *doors*
двухме́стный *double*
  *(room)*
де́вушка *waitress, girl,*
де́душка (m.)
  *grandfather*
дела́ *things;* как у вас
дела́? *how are you?*
  *(formal)*
де́лать *to do, make:*
  де́лать переса́дку
  *to change (trains)*
день (m.) *day:* на
ско́лько дней? *for how*
  *many days?* на два дня
  *for two days*
десе́рт *dessert*
де́ти *children*
джин *gin*
дипло́м *diploma*
до *to, up to, as far as*
до свида́ния *goodbye*

до́лларами *with dollars*
дом *house*
дорого́й (m.) дорога́я
  *(f.)* дорого́е (n.) *dear*
дочь (f.) *daughter*
друг *friend (m.)*
душ *shower:*
  с ду́шем *with a shower*
дя́дя (m.) *uncle*

## Ее

его́ *him:*
  как его́ зову́т? *what's*
  *his name?*
  у него́ есть *he has*
её *her:*
  как её зову́т? *what's her*
  *name?*
  у неё есть *she has*
есть *there is*
есть *to eat*
ещё *more, still:*
  что ещё? *anything else?*

## Жж

жа́реный (m.) жа́реная
  (f.) жа́реное (n.) *fried,*
  *roasted*
жена́ *wife*
жена́т (m.) *married (man;*
  *informal)* жена́ты (m.)
  *married (man; formal)*
жест *gesture*
жето́н *token (metro)*
(вы) живёте (жить)
  *(you) live (formal)*
(ты) живёшь (жить)
  *(you) live (informal)*
(я) живу́ (жить) *(I) live,*
  *stay*

## Зз

заказа́ть *to book:*
  я заказа́л (m.)
  я заказа́ла (f.) *I've*
  *booked*

закрыва́ются
(закрыва́ться)
  *(they) close, shut:*
  две́ри закрыва́ются *the*
  *doors are closing*
закры́т (m.) закры́та (f.)
  закры́то (n.) *closed, shut*
заку́ски *starters,*
  *appetizers*
за́мужем (f.) *married*
  *(woman)*
здесь *here*
здра́вствуй *hello*
  *(informal)* здра́вствуйте
  *hello (formal)*
(я) зна́ю (знать) *(I) know*
зову́т (звать) *(they) call:*
  как вас зову́т? *what's*
  *your name?*

## Ии

и *and*
идёт (идти́) *(it) goes*
  иди́те (идти́) *(you –*
  *formal or pl.) go*
икра́ *caviar*
и́ли *or*
инжене́р *engineer*
Интури́ст *Intourist*
  *(travel firm)*
информа́ция *information*
Ирла́ндия *Ireland*
Испа́ния *Spain*
ита́к *so*
Ита́лия *Italy*

## Кк

как *how*
како́й? (m.) кака́я? (f.)
  како́е? (n.) каки́е? (pl.)
  *which?*
  на како́м этаже́? *on*
  *which floor?*
Кана́да *Canada*
кана́дец (m.) *Canadian*
Ка́нберра *Canberra*
карп *carp*
ка́рта *map, card:*

креди́тной ка́ртой *by credit card*
карто́фель (m.) *potatoes:*
  с карто́фелем *with potatoes*
ка́сса *cash-desk*
кафе́ *café*
кварти́ра *flat*
квас *soft drink made from black bread and yeast*
Ки́ев *Kiev*
килогра́мм *kilogram(me)*
киломе́тр *kilometre*
кино́ *cinema*
кио́ск *kiosk*
ключ *key*
когда́ *when*
колбаса́ *sausage (salami)*
коли́чество *number, amount*
ко́ма *coma*
коме́та *comet*
кому́ *to whom*
коне́ц *end:*
  в оди́н коне́ц *single (ticket)*
коне́чно *of course*
контро́льная рабо́та *checkpoint*
конце́рт *concert*
конья́к *cognac, brandy*
копе́йка *kopeck:*
  две копе́йки *2 kopecks,* шесть копе́ек *6 kopecks*
кото́рый? (m.) кото́рая? (f.) кото́рое? (n.) *which?, what?*
  в кото́ром часу́? *(at) what time?*
ко́фе *coffee*
краси́вый (m.) *beautiful*
кра́сный (m.) кра́сная (f.) кра́сное (n.) *red*
креди́тной ка́ртой *with a/by credit card*
Кремль (m.) *Kremlin*
куда́? *where (to)?*
купи́ть *to buy*

ку́рица *chicken*
курс *course*
ку́хня *cooking*

## Лл

лимо́н *lemon:*
  с лимо́ном *with lemon*
лимона́д *lemonade*
литр *litre*
лифт *lift, elevator*
ло́жки *spoons*
Ло́ндон *London*
люкс *luxury*

## Мм

магази́н *shop*
Макдо́нальдс *Macdonald's*
ма́ма *mum, mummy*
Манче́стер *Manchester*
ма́рка *stamp:*
  почто́вая ма́рка *postage stamp*
ма́сло *oil, butter:*
  в ма́сле *in oil*
матрёшка *set of Russian dolls*
матч *match (sport)*
мать (f.) *mother*
ме́дленно *slowly*
меню́ *menu*
меня́ *me*
  у меня́ есть *I have*
  меня́ зову́т *my name is*
ме́сто *place*
метрдоте́ль (m.) *head waiter*
метро́ *metro, underground*
минера́льная вода́ *mineral water*
Минск *Minsk*
мину́та *minute*
мне *(to) me:*
  да́йте мне *give me*
мо́жно *it's possible, yes, you may, OK*

мой (m.) моя́ (f.) моё (n.) *my*
молодо́й (m.) молода́я (f.) молодо́е (n.) *young:*
  молодо́й челове́к *waiter*
молоко́ *milk:*
  с молоко́м *with milk,* без молока́ *without milk*
моро́женое *ice cream*
Москва́ *Moscow*
москви́ч (m.) москви́чка (f.) *Muscovite*
муж *husband*
музе́й *museum*
мя́со *meat*

## Нн

на *on, to, for*
на́до *it's necessary*
нале́во *(to) left*
напи́тки *drinks*
напра́во *(to) right*
натура́льный (m.) натура́льная (f.) натура́льное (n.) *natural:*
  бифште́кс натура́льный *grilled beefsteak*
национа́льный (m.) национа́льная (f.) национа́льное (n.) *national:*
  национа́льные блю́да *national dishes*
не *not*
него́ *him:*
  у него́ есть *he has*
недалеко́ *not far*
неё *her:*
  у неё есть *she has*
нет *no, there isn't, there aren't*
ничего́ *nothing, never mind, not bad*
Но́вгород *Novgorod*
но́мер *room, number, size, item*
норма́льно *normally:* всё

нормáльно? *is everything all right?*

нрáвится (нрáвиться) *like:* мне нрáвится *I like (it),* мне нрáвятся *I like (them)*

Нью-Йóрк *New York*

## Оо

обрáтно *back:* тудá и обрáтно *return (ticket)*

объéкт *object*

Одéсса *Odessa*

одúн (m.) однá (f.) однó (n.) *one*

одномéстныи (m.) *single (room)*

он *he, it (m.)*

онá *she, it (f.)*

онú *they*

онó *it (n.)*

оплатúть *to pay*

оркéстр *orchestra, live band*

останóвка *stop (bus, tram)*

осторóжно *take care, be careful*

отéц *father*

открыт (m.), открыта (f.), открыто (n.) *open*

открытка *postcard*

отправлéние *departure*

отхóдит (отходúть) *leave*

óчень *very*

## Пп

пакéт *packet, carton*

пáпа *dad, daddy*

парк *park*

пáспорт *passport*

пéпси-кóла *coke*

пéрвый (m.) пéрвая (f.) пéрвое (n.) *first:* пéрвое *first course;* пéрвые блюда *first courses;*

на пéрвом этажé *on the first floor*

пересáдка *change:* дéлать пересáдку *to (make a) change (train)*

пешкóм *on foot*

пúво *beer*

пирожкú *pasties, small pies:* с пирожкáми *with pasties, small pies*

пить *to drink*

план *map, plan*

платúте (платúть) *pay*

платфóрма *platform:* с какóй платфóрмы? *from which platform?*

плóщадь (f.) *square*

повторúйте (повторúть) *repeat*

подрýга *friend (f.)*

пóезд *train*

пожáлуйста *please, don't mention it, here you are*

полкилó *half a kilo*

помидóры *tomatoes*

понедéльник *Monday*

(я) понимáю (понимáть) *(I) understand*

пообéдать *to dine*

по-рýсски *in Russian*

посмотрéть *to look (at)*

потóм *then*

пóчта *post office*

почтóвая мáрка *postage stamp*

прибытие *arrival*

привéт *regards, greetings*

приятного аппетúта *enjoy your meal*

проспéкт *avenue, boulevard*

простúте (простúть) *excuse me, sorry*

прямо *straight on*

пятница *Friday:* в пятницу *on Friday*

## Рр

рабóта *work*

рад (m.) рáда (f.) *glad, pleased*

(вы) рекомендýете (рекомендовáть) *recommend*

ресторáн *restaurant*

рúс *rice:* с рúсом *with rice*

ром *rum*

Россúя *Russia:* в Россúи *in Russia*

рубль (m.) *rouble:* три рубля *3 roubles,* пять рублéй *5 roubles*

рýсский (m.) рýсская (f.) рýсское (n.) рýсские (pl) *Russian:* по-рýсски *in Russian*

рыба *fish*

рынок *market:* на рынке *at the market*

## Сс

с, со *with, from*

салáт *salad*

самовáр *samovar*

Санкт-Петербýрг *St Petersburg*

сардúны *sardines*

сáуна *sauna*

сáхар *sugar:* с сáхаром *with sugar,* без сáхара *without sugar*

свобóдный *free*

сдáча *change (money returned)*

сегóдня *today*

сéрвис-бюрó *service desk*

сестрá *sister*

скажúте (сказáть) *tell (me), excuse me*

скóлько? *how much, how many?*

слáдкий (m.) слáдкая (f.) слáдкое (n.) *sweet*

сла́дкое *sweet course*
сле́дующий (m.)
сле́дующая (f.)
сле́дующее (n.) *next*
слу́шаю (слу́шать) *listen:*
слу́шаю вас *at your service*
смета́на *sour cream:*
в смета́не *in sour cream,*
со смета́ной *with sour cream*
сок *juice*
спаси́бо *thank you*
спра́вочное бюро́ *enquiry office*
среда́ *Wednesday:*
в сре́ду *on Wednesday*
ста́нция *station (metro)*
сто́ит (сто́ить) *costs:*
ско́лько сто́ит? *how much does it cost?,*
ско́лько сто́ят? *how much do they cost?*
стоя́нка *stand, rank (taxi)*
студе́нт (m.), студе́нтка (f.) *student*
суббо́та *Saturday:*
в суббо́ту *on Saturday*
сувени́ры *souvenirs*
суп *soup*
суперма́ркет *supermarket*
сухо́й (m.) суха́я (f.)
сухо́е (n.) *dry*
схе́ма *plan:*
схе́ма метро́ *plan of the metro*
счёт *bill*
съезд *congress*
сын *son*
сыр *cheese*

## Тт
та́кже *also*
такси́ *taxi*
такт *tact*
тало́н *travel coupon, ticket*

твой (m.) твоя́ (f.)
твоё (n.) *your (informal)*
теа́тр *theatre*
тебе́ *(to) you (informal):*
тебе́ нра́вится? *do you like (it)?*
тебя́ *you (informal):*
как тебя́ зову́т? *what's your name?*
телефо́н *telephone*
тётя *aunt*
то́лько *only*
тома́т *tomato sauce:*
в тома́те *in tomato sauce*
тома́тный *tomato:*
тома́тный сок *tomato juice*
торт *cake*
традицио́нный (m.)
традицио́нная (f.)
традицио́нное (n.) *traditional:*
традицио́нная ку́хня *traditional cooking*
тра́ктор *tractor*
трамва́й *tram*
тре́тий (m.) тре́тья (f.)
тре́тье (n.) *third:*
на тре́тьем этаже́ *on the third floor*
тролле́йбус *trolleybus:*
тролле́йбусом *by trolleybus*
туале́т *toilet*
туда́ *(to) there:*
туда́ и обра́тно *return (ticket)*
ты *you (informal)*

## Уу
у вас есть? *have you got? (formal)* Как у вас дела́? *How are you? (formal)*
уго́дно: что вам уго́дно? *what would you like?*
Узбекиста́н *Uzbekistan*
Украи́на *Ukraine*

у́лица *street:*
на у́лице *in the street,*
универма́г *department store*
универса́м *self-service shop*
университе́т *university*
уха́ *fish soup*
Уэ́льс *Wales*

## Фф
фами́лия *surname*
фа́нта *Fanta, fizzy orange*
фотоаппара́т *camera*
Фра́нция *France*
фру́кты *fruit:*
с фру́ктами *with fruit*
фу́нтами *with pounds (sterling)*

## Хх
хара́ктер *character*
хлеб *bread*
холо́дный (m.)
холо́дная (f.)
холо́дное (n.) *cold*
хорошо́ *fine, good, well, OK*
(вы) хоти́те (хоте́ть) *(you — formal) want*
(ты) хо́чешь (хоте́ть) *(you — informal) want*

## Цц
центр *centre*

## Чч
чай *tea*
час *hour:*
в кото́ром часу́? *(at) what time?* два часа́ *2 o'clock,* семь часо́в *7 o'clock*
чек *receipt*
челове́к *person, people*
чёрный (m.), чёрная (f.)
чёрное (n.) *black*
четве́рг *Thursday*

что? *what?*

## Шш
шампа́нское *champagne*
ша́пка *hat, cap*
шашлы́к *shashlyk, kebab*
шко́льница *schoolgirl*
Шотла́ндия *Scotland*

## Щщ
щи *cabbage soup*
щу́ка *pike*

## Ээ
экза́мен *examination*
экспе́рт *expert*
Эрмита́ж *Hermitage*
эта́ж *floor, storey:*
  на како́м этаже́? *on
  which floor?*
э́то *this, that, it (is)*

## Яя
я *I*
я́блоки *apples*
Я́лта *Yalta*

# Now you're talking

## Russian Language & People

*Russian Language & People* is the ideal next step to *Talk Russian*. As well as teaching the skills necessary to communicate in and understand Russian, it provides an accessible introduction to the written language, along with fascinating insights into modern Russia and traditional customs.

■ **192pp course book**
■ **2 x audio CDs**

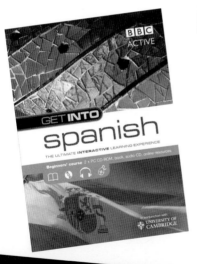

If you'd like to start speaking other languages, from Spanish to Mandari Chinese, BBC Active offers a wide choice of innovative resources to help you. Designed by language-teaching experts, our courses range from audio-only to interactive CD-ROMS, for beginners and the more advanced.

We also publish a series of phrasebooks and guides to gramma